Self-esteem Games

JOHN WILEY & SONS, INC.

New York · Chichester · Weinheim · Brisbane · Singapore · Toronto

Self-esteem Games

300 Fun Activities That Make Children Feel Good about Themselves

BARBARA SHER

ILLUSTRATIONS BY
RALPH BUTLER

Published by John Wiley & Sons, Inc.
Published simultaneously in Canada.

This publication is designed to provide accurate and authoritative information in regard to the subject matter covered. It is sold with the understanding that the publisher is not engaged in rendering professional services. If professional advice or other expert assis-tance is required, the services of a competent professional person should be sought.

Library of Congress Cataloging-in-Publication Data:
Sher, Barbara.
    Self-esteem games : 300 fun activities that make children feel good
   about themselves / Barbara Sher.
       p.   cm.
   Includes index.
   ISBN 0–471–18027–0 (pbk. : alk. paper)
    1. Family recreation.   2. Self-esteem in children.   I. Title.
GV182.8.S44   1998
793—cd21   98–14670

Printed in the United States of America
10 9 8

To Marissa, Roxanne, and Richard,
with enormous love

Acknowledgments

I thank my editor, Carole Hall, for her careful work and jolly conversations.

I thank Diane Aronson and Miriam Sarzin for being such capable members of the editorial team.

I thank Ralph Butler for capturing the fun in his illustrations.

I thank my agent, Judi Schuler, for being a superb ally.

I thank my friends and family for their exceptional support.

And, I thank all the many children who have played these games and shared their joy with me.

Contents ‿ ‿ ‿ ‿ ‿ ‿ ‿ ‿ ‿ ‿ ‿ ‿

Self-esteem Games

Introduction ⸱ ⸍ ⸌ ⸍ ⸌ ⸍ ⸌ ⸍ ⸌ ⸍ ⸌

ENCOURAGING THE SENSE OF SELF

Children are the flowers of our lives, each one a unique variation on nature's theme. The self-esteem games in this book offer hundreds of happy ways to help children bloom and flourish.

Nature encourages variation. Look closely at a host of daffodils. You'll see that they are as individual as fingerprints. One has a deeper yellow, another tiny white streaks, and another an extra petal. Even the leaves on their stems are different from each other. They are easily identifiable by their shape and color. But look more closely and you'll see that each leaf has different vein lines or perhaps a nibbled spot caused by a passing insect, an added bump from a friendly fungus, or a beginning brittleness.

Self-esteem games show children that it is okay to be themselves, because the essence of self-esteem is to know and accept who we are just as we are now—not a begrudging acceptance, as in "This is as good as we can get," but a satisfying appreciation, as in "This is who we are, this is the unique sound of our notes on the keyboard of humanity."

Children are not objects that we can change to our specifications, any more than a seed can become any other flower but what it is. Our job is not to make our children into what we want, but rather to help them grow into what they are.

My friend Donald, in his sixties, exemplified this attitude beautifully when someone asked him how he was doing in ballet class. "I am no Baryshnikov," he replied, pulling himself up to his full, proud height, "but neither is he me!"

Recently, I saw a bumper sticker that read, "Be unique like everyone else!" This book encourages that kind of positive self-image. Not only does

1

it make life more enjoyable, it provides a foundation for learning. If children don't feel good about themselves, how can they open up to learning new things that might expose their weaknesses? Educators agree. Self-esteem gives us the ability to take risks, learn from the results, and move on.

MY PERSONAL STORY

When I was a child, my father had an expression he used lovingly and often. "As long as it makes you happy," he'd say. It was his ultimate guideline for any decision.

I became an occupational therapist with a graduate degree, and as I grew older, I would follow my happiness and leave a well-paying position in the city, move to a remote country setting and work mainly with children from low-income homes, sometimes bartering my fee. There I met the man with whom I would build a house and homebirth and raise two daughters.

As it turned out, my choices were the right ones for me and led me on paths I had only dreamed about. I found a way of living that made me happy—writing books and helping children to increase their physical and mental skills. Because neither I nor the families I worked with had excess cash, I became interested in playing therapeutic and educational games that did not require expensive equipment.

My books brought me invitations to travel internationally, to give workshops and share knowledge with wonderful people. I worked on a lovely Micronesian island for a year and a half, bringing my family with me. These experiences gave me lots of time to spend in relaxed family life, enjoying my kids and the world around us, whether in the forest, at home, or on mountains beyond our shores.

I followed my father's advice, and chose a path that made me feel happy. I found my own uniqueness. This has made all the difference.

FOR YOUR CHILD'S HAPPINESS AND SELF-ESTEEM

The games and activities in this book help children appreciate being unique, get to know themselves, and feel good about sharing who they are. Let's take a look at why each of these goals matters.

Being Unique!

Self-esteem games help children appreciate their own specialness at any age (or never to doubt it in the first place). All children need lots of feedback about their uniqueness. They need to know that whatever things they enjoy doing the most are just fine. Most of the time, we give them this feedback in everyday comments like these:

"I notice that you are especially sweet to small animals and they seem to be drawn to you, too."

"Dad and I were talking about your love of puzzles when we were at the store, so we brought you these new ones."

"You use such serene, quiet colors in that picture. I feel comforted just looking at it."

"Gosh, you are such a good shopper. You always find the best deals."

"Using your body full-out must really be good for you; I noticed you always seem happier after you've been shooting baskets for a while."

The games we play with our children reinforce the idea that we value their choices and their skills. Our children don't need to share our preferences any more than we need to share theirs. We do need to respect their choices. Some children enjoy being with groups. Others are happier being solitary. Some enjoy physical sports. Others would rather sit alone and write. One preference is not better or worse than the other. They are just different.

Appreciating yourself is not always easy—at any age. One day, my daughter Roxanne came home after her small rural class had taken a field trip to visit a larger town school and asked sadly, "No matter how pretty I think I am, there is someone prettier and no matter how smart I think I am, there always is someone smarter! How can I ever be the best?" We agreed that the answer was to be uniquely herself. No one could ever be Roxanne as well as she could. We made a list of all the things she enjoyed so she could follow her own interests.

It is easier to appreciate yourself if you have interests, looks, and skills people in your environment praise, but difficult and more important work if you don't.

Children often learn this the hard way. For example, a young person who went to Portugal as an exchange student noticed that most of the Portuguese girls had curly hair. She wanted so much to be valued that the first thing she did was get a curly permanent so that she would look more like the other girls. She later realized that it was her former straight hair, not curly, that people most admired in this culture because it was more unusual.

Appreciating one's uniqueness is part of self-love. As we increase our capacity to love ourselves, we increase our capacity to love others. This is a necessary step toward peace, both in ourselves, and in the world.

Getting to Know Me!

Self-esteem games teach children to trust their feeling sense. Too often, we encourage them to do just the opposite. A cry of "I hate my brother" is often answered with, "No, you don't."

"Sounds like you're feeling some hate for him right now. You must be really mad at him (if the child looks angry), or "It looks as if your feelings are hurt" (if the child looks sad) would be more validating.

I was watching an infant in a car seat recently. When his mother got out of the car, his face contorted with the look of panic and worry. When she came around and opened his door, his face shone with immense joy and delight. It brought home to me the fact that children really do have the same range of emotional responses as we do. In this situation, we may think that the baby overreacted. From his perspective, however, the response was completely appropriate.

Our job, as I see it, is to help our children notice and name their emotional states, not necessarily to "make it all better." We can't always cure them of sadness or make them stop being angry, but we can listen and understand, and that is a big help.

My youngest daughter, Marissa, taught me that lesson well. She was about five at the time and was looking unusually "down."

"What is wrong, Marissa?" I asked.

"None of my wishes will ever come true," she replied sadly.

"Tell me what you want, maybe I can help," I said in my omnipotent parent way. All the while, I was thinking, What could it be that I can't fix with a new toy or a tray of hot-from-the-oven chocolate chip cookies?

She said, "You can't help. I want a kitten that will never grow up. I want a Christmas tree that will never grow old and I want my mom and dad to never die." She was right. Sometimes we can't make things better. Sometimes we can only commiserate.

Giving children permission to talk about their emotions without fear of being censured gives them the self-esteem to know their feelings matter.

Sharing Who I Am!

It's one thing to get to know yourself and listen to others; it's quite another to be brave enough to share yourself with others. Sharing your thoughts and feelings opens you up to the risk of rejection or misunderstanding.

Ah, but to be understood—to have one person or many persons know just what you mean and feel the same way or, at the least, love you anyway—that is worth the risk.

In order to believe that they are okay as they are, children need to know that they are always growing. What they accomplish does not matter as much as who they are inside. Self-esteem games help children see each other—their similarities and their differences—in a new light.

Our best accomplishment, our most creative work, is our own person—how we act, how we treat others, how we are. We are our own best product. To paraphrase Mother Teresa, "More important than doing great things is to do little things with great love."

GETTING READY TO PLAY

In this book you will find hundreds of games and activities that will give you many happy hours of playtime with your child. Here are a few things that it will help to know in advance:

> ▶ Almost all of these games are fun for children of all ages. Games that work especially well for children under five are coded with a 👤 .

▶ All of the games can be played with children of either sex, regardless of the gender of the children in the instructions or illustrations.

▶ Almost all of the games can be played by two willing players—you and your child.

▶ If the instructions of an intriguing game are written for a group, remember that you can always modify the rules a bit to fit just the two of you.

▶ Some of the games work especially well with groups. These games are coded with a ◯. If you have a growing family, are a classroom teacher or volunteer, a playgroup leader, a camp counselor—or are organizing a birthday party or a family gathering—you will enjoy playing around with these ideas. Games that work well with large groups can be found mainly in chapter 8.

▶ Chant and song games are played in rondo fashion. Players repeat a short chant together and then an individual responds before the group repeats the chant. Play continues until everyone has given his or her response. If there are just two of you playing, you have lots of turns each!

▶ Chant and song games create a friendly atmosphere, engaging the more intuitive right side of the brain. Each person has a moment to take a breath before responding, and the person who just had a turn has a moment to reflect on his or her success.

▶ Chants make good songs! It's fun to make up simple tunes on your piano or guitar.

▶ It can be helpful to explain to kids that sometimes we feel a moment of discomfort before it is our turn to respond. It's nice to know that others feel a certain amount of social angst regardless of how "cool" they might act. What the games show us is that we can trust ourselves to come up with something.

▶ Remember there are no wrong answers. Any response is okay, even if it's nonsensical. Silence can be just right, too.

▶ There are many variations of some of the games because learning the same lessons in many ways makes them "stick to the ribs" better. Also, discovering different ways to learn the same things increases a child's acceptance of variations. There is more than one path to self-esteem!

The best setting for the various games is always the same: a playful, safe place where being oneself is the best thing to be.

Although I write in English, children who speak other languages also enjoy the games. I have played them in Vietnam, Cambodia, and Laos; with students in Hong Kong, Fiji, and Rarotonga; and with teachers in New Zealand (both Maori and European). Many, many children in the United States, from Headstart preschoolers to sixth graders and teens, have also been game players. I have led play workshops with Native Americans from many different Indian nations. Everywhere, there were lots of smiles, plus laughs, and very good feelings. One person in Cambodia told me, through an interpreter, "My mouth hurts from smiling so much!"

Play, I have found, is the universal language. It's fun for everyone to have fun.

THE BEST TIME TO PLAY

We have only a brief while to establish a positive influence over our children's lives. Seize the moments while your children are young, and leave the dishes and laundry for later.

The best time to play is whenever the mood strikes you. On a rainy day, when friends are over, when you want to linger a little longer around the dinner table, at birthday parties, or instead of TV, play a game. When you are driving in the car and want to distract siblings from their arguments or their complaints about being bored, play a game. Play when your children are in a high-energy mood on one of your low-energy days.

Pick the game that fits the mood. You might want to have a regular game time that the children can count on.

Browse through and see which games appeal to you and jot down the titles and page numbers. Stick your list on the refrigerator to help you remember.

I admit I am a bit of a gamesmeister, and I think I am passing on this trait. Recently, my daughters were home from college and doing their laundry. Faced with a pile of seemingly mismatched single socks, they lightened the moment by spontaneously playing our childhood game of Go Fish. They started by dealing out a "hand" of six socks each.

"Anyone have a blue pair with a green stripe?" asked Marissa.

"Nope, go fish," said Roxanne.

Now it's your turn.

PART ONE

Being Unique!

Chapter 1

KNOWING MY STRENGTHS

Children five and under know lots of things they do well. Older children are less certain, having met others who do things even better. A group of kindergartners were asked, "Who can draw?" Every hand shot up. When that same question was asked of second graders, only a few hesitant hands were raised. These games remind children of all the good things they can do—even if you're the one to remind them.

Things I Do Well

CHANT

> Here are things that I do well, I do well, I do well.
> Here are things that I do well.
> Do you do them, too?

RESPONSE

> I can _____

Example

I can ride a two-wheeler!

DIRECTIONS

Chant together between each person's turn. Each player gets to name something they do well. Start by taking your turn first to demonstrate how the game works. Take several turns if your child needs help getting started.

Nicknames

Children can either give themselves a nickname they would like or the family can think of one for them. Only positive images are acceptable. We get enough of the other kind from the outside world.

CHANT

Dimples, Sharp Eyes, and Mr. Fame.

Now, what is *your* nickname?

RESPONSE

My nickname is _____

Example

My nickname is FLASH! I'm fast.

Animal-Steem

CHANT

If I were an animal, I would be

Someone

Just like me!

RESPONSE

If I were an animal, I would be a _____
Because it's good at _____,
Just like me!

Example

If I were an animal, I would be an otter
Because it's good at playing,
Just like me!

VARIATIONS

♦ Act out the animal. There is something wonderful about a child seeing Mom or another adult acting like a chimpanzee or goat or an aardvark!

♦ Name another quality in an animal you admire. You're likely to find that the quality admired is one the player has, even if that player is not aware of it or has not fully developed it yet. You might hear:

> *"I like the bear because it's strong."*

> *"I like the mountain goat because it's agile."*

> *"I like the dolphins because they can relate to other species."*

Clown Walk

You can create a clown character and learn something about yourself at the same time. If you tend to walk with your pelvis slightly tilted back in a sway-back position, exaggerate that look. If you tend to walk with your chin slightly tilted up, exaggerate that look, too. Add them together and you will discover a walk that is a unique, funny exaggeration of your own.

DIRECTIONS

Show your child your funny clown walk. Invite him to walk around with you and invent his own clown walk, too. While he is walking, say:

◇ Is your weight on your heels, toes, or the inside or outside of your feet? Exaggerate it!

◇ Is your pelvis tilted forward or backward? Exaggerate it!

◇ How are your arms moving—a lot, a little? Exaggerate it!

◇ How big are your steps—small, large? Exaggerate them!

◇ Are your shoulders up toward your ears or hunched forward? Exaggerate it!

◇ Chin down? Chin up? Exaggerate it!

◇ Are you looking down or up? Exaggerate it!

VARIATIONS

◆ Give your clowns names that feel right such as Macho, Miss Sunshine, or Walking Fear. Also try naming each other's clowns.

◆ Imitate each other's walks. Feel what it is like to be in the other person's shoes!

Pal-of-the-Day

A little one-room schoolhouse I know has a big idea. Every week someone pulls a child's name out of a hat. That person gets his or her body outlined on a large piece of paper and colored in by the group. Next to the outline, the teacher writes down comments elicited from the class:

"I like her laugh."

"She is always nice to be with."

"She's my best friend."

I've seen one of those pictures hanging in a child's room long after she outgrew the school. Nicona, a five-year-old boy, told me months later, word for word, what each child said about him.

DIRECTIONS

Choose a person-of-the-day in your family. Schedule one day each week, Sunday for example, to draw one of your names out of a hat. Adults get a turn, too!

The chosen person gets to do anything that she particularly likes. She can drink milkshakes, go to the zoo, visit the library, play video games, or lie around the house eating cherries. If anyone complains, remind them that everyone will have a turn (or make other arrangements for them).

Of course, the chosen person gets her "portrait" drawn by lying down on a big piece of paper and having her body outlined and then colored in by the rest of the family. Remember, everyone gets to write a friendly comment on the paper.

Put this event on the family calendar so it doesn't get "spaced out!"

Materials

Shelf-liner paper or butcher paper, crayons

VARIATION

◆ Let the person-of-the-day choose an event for everyone to do together that day, like going to the movies or to the beach.

The Ways I Am Smart

Children are smart in different ways. Mathematical and verbal intelligence are measured on IQ tests. Now, other aspects of intelligence are being recognized, such as intrapersonal (knowing yourself), interpersonal (understanding others), and kinesthetic (knowing your body).

DIRECTIONS

Ask players to write down the ways in which they are smart or skilled. Family members might want to add to each other's lists.

Examples

◇ *Mom's List*   I can recognize when I am upset and need some quiet time alone to sort out my thoughts.

My friends say I am a good listener and like to share their thoughts with me.

I remember to say nice things to myself when I've just done something stupid. Things like, "Well at least you tried!"

◇ *Kara's List*   I am really good at catching a ball.

All the kids want me on their team.

I am a good sport and cheer my friends on.

I pick up new sports easily.

I like to read.

Magic Words

Hearing nice things said about you can brighten up a day. It's like magic.

DIRECTIONS

Write down a list of positive adjectives that might describe someone else. You can start with the list below and then add your own words.

Then have each player add to your list or make their own. Players can fatten each other's lists. You will probably hear some slang from your kids, such as awesome, rad, or whatever words are "in." (Other countries and cultures have their own words. My English friends say "wicked" or "brilliant" when describing something great.)

Here's my starter list:

Kind, happy, silly, robust, outgoing, vivacious, dreamy, daring, bold, assertive, tough, careful, talkative, loyal, sensitive, creative, adventurous, generous, funny, boisterous, calm, quiet, studious.

Materials

Pins, pencils, paper

VARIATION

◆ You can make a list of more negative adjectives, and players can add to those, too. After all, you can't fix something if you don't know it's broken. Point out positive alternatives for the negative words, whenever possible. Nosy is also inquisitive. Impatient is also excited, and so on.

Here are some words to start with:

Nosy (inquisitive), suspicious (skeptical), fearful (cautious), selfish (self-oriented), sloppy (casual).

Players make lists of words that describe how they see themselves. Pin your lists to your shirts so others can't read them. Then pin a blank sheet of paper on each person's back. On that paper, players write positive words that describe the person.

Compare your private words with the words the others wrote.

Spin the Bottle

You might be familiar with this game from your own childhood. Maybe you got your first kiss playing this game. In this version, the kisses are verbal ones. Sometimes that silly bottle will keep pointing at the same person. You can go with that or cheat and move the bottle toward the person who has not had a turn yet. I cheat.

DIRECTIONS

Materials
Bottle

Sit in a circle or facing each other and spin a bottle that is lying on its side. When the bottle stops spinning, the neck will be pointing toward one of you. The spinner then says something positive about that person, even if she herself is the one the bottle is pointing to. It can be a story, a pleasant memory, or a quality she admires or envies.

You may need to give young children a sentence to finish such as "When I see <u>(name of child bottle is pointing at)</u>, what makes me smile inside is _____."

Compliments

Accepting sincere praise can be hard, particularly when the attributes you take for granted (for example, being kind and funny) are the ones that others are praising.

*After each turn, ask the receiver of the compliment if someone said some-
thing that was surprising. Ask what they liked or didn't like about being the
center of attention.*

DIRECTIONS

Face each other or sit in a circle. Take turns giving each other a compliment. It can be as simple as, "You're wearing a pretty dress" or as profound
as "You have a quiet strength about you that is a source of comfort to me."

If compliments seem uncomfortable to give, just say something such
as, "I noticed you like to play ball" or "I noticed you always wear that interesting bracelet."

You will want to move fast enough so that there is a minimum of awk-
wardness, but slow enough so that each person really "hears" what is being
said.

VARIATION

♦ If you write down the compliments that you receive, you will work
harder at listening to what is being said. Sit with your child and write
them down together as you say them.

Birthday Favors

*Birthday compliments help the celebrant to recognize the accomplishments
of another year. Your child may hardly remember all that others said, but
will remember feeling appreciated.*

DIRECTIONS

Everyone celebrating the occasion puts a candle on the cake. As he lights it,
he describes how knowing the birthday person is helpful or whatever other
nice thing he feels like saying to the birthday person. (Optional: Tape
record the occasion so your child can replay it whenever he wants.)

Materials

Birthday cake,
candles, tape
recorder
(optional)

Silhouettes

Make silhouettes of each family member and hang them up next to each other to reinforce the ways each person is unique as well as similar.

Materials

Paper, crayon or marker, magazines, paste

DIRECTIONS

Have your child face sideways between a light and a wall. This will cause her profile to appear on the wall, where you have cleverly placed a paper so you can outline the shadow and produce a silhouette of her head.

VARIATIONS

♦ Go through magazines and catalogs with your child and cut out pictures of things you each like to think about. Paste those pictures around the heads of your silhouettes.

♦ Do one of each family member and pin them up side by side. Talk about the similarities and the differences, appreciating them all!

Fingers and Toes

Sit with your child and pore over magazine pictures together. I guarantee you a lovely afternoon. "Look at this picture of a beach. You make the most wonderful sand castles. Should we cut this one out?"

DIRECTIONS

Place your child's hands on a piece of paper and outline them. Have him do the same with your hands, if he is able. Now go through old catalogs and magazines and find things you like to do with your hands. Cut out the pictures and paste them around your outlines.

Do the same activity with each other's feet. Outline them on a piece of paper and then find pictures that remind you of things that your own feet like to do or places they like to go.

Materials

Paper, crayon or marker, magazines, paste

Fingerprints

Fingerprints have always been the absolute proof that each of us is one-of-a-kind (much to the regret of many a criminal).

DIRECTIONS

Using an ink pad, help your child make a print of his index finger on an index card. Then make a print of your own. Take turns noticing the differences.

Outline a whole hand and make a fingerprint for each finger. Place the prints in the hand outline so children can see that even each finger of their hand is unique!!

VARIATION

♦ In a group, play a game in which everyone makes a fingerprint card. Place the cards face down. Each person picks a card and tries to identify whose print it is, explaining why. The reasons can be hilarious!

Materials

Ink pad, index cards

Treasured

This game is especially fun to play in groups. Follow all announcements of accomplishments by rousing cheers.

DIRECTIONS

Take turns being treasured. The others face the "treasured person" while you announce that this wonderful, incredible person just single-handedly achieved one of the following (pick one below). One by one, everyone walks up to the treasured person and gives a genuine pat on the back, or a hug and a kiss, or words of praise or gratefulness.

Possible fantasy accomplishments

◊ Obtained a nuclear freeze

◊ Cured AIDS

◊ Saved the spotted owl

◊ Stopped the destruction of the rain forest

◊ Ended all wars

◊ Thought of a new way to recycle car tires

◊ Built a better mousetrap

Possible real accomplishments

◊ Fixed his mother breakfast when she was sick

◊ Kept her handwriting all on the same line

◊ Gave his brother a ride home on his bike

◊ Remembered to turn in her math paper

◊ Stayed up all night with a sick friend

◊ Was especially helpful to his father

◊ Washed the dishes without being told

◊ Helped her best friend do her chores.

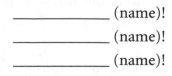

Hero

DIRECTIONS

Invite your child to act out the fantasy or true-life hero or heroine of his or her choice. Maybe it's a soccer player carried on the shoulders of admiring fans who are grateful for the winning score.

Perhaps it's a dad who built a puppet theater for his kids' school, and hears a round of "For he's a jolly good fellow."

Join in the fantasy. Be the roaring crowd that gives a hug, sings the song, or lifts the hero onto its shoulders.

Just for Being You

We need to be sure to show that we appreciate our children's essence, not just their external accomplishments. Being ourselves and being kind and considerate of others to the best of our own nature are major accomplishments, too. I know it would make my day if someone yelled out this cheer for me: "Barbara, Barbara, Barbara!!!!!!" Try it with your child.

CHANT

2, 4, 6, 8
Who do we appreciate?
1, 3, 5, 9
Who do we think is mighty fine?

RESPONSE

_____ (name)!
_____ (name)!
_____ (name)!

Mirror, Mirror

I had just gone through a very intense creative time. Exhausted, but pleased that all had gone well, I looked in the mirror, smiled lovingly at myself, and said, "Good job!"

A shocking thing happened. I realized that the person in the mirror had never looked at me like that before. I was used to frowning at my hair when it had a mind of its own or poking at blemishes or acknowledging a new wrinkle. This smiling person with love shining out of her eyes had a face that my children must see when they insist that to them I am beautiful.

Now, I make a point of smiling lovingly at myself regardless of my flaws. Immediately, I feel and look better.

Materials

Large mirror

DIRECTIONS

Look in the mirror with your child and practice making different faces together. First, try problem faces: look angry, look surprised, look frightened, look disgusted, look worried. When you make those faces notice the lines formed with each expression like a paper you have folded and refolded in the same places.

Now smile at yourself with the utmost sincerity. If you have any problem with giving yourself this much love, think of someone you dearly love. Then give that openhearted love to yourself. Your face may have blemishes, lines, or crows feet, but I bet you look great!!

VARIATIONS

◆ Say kind words to yourself in the mirror—congratulations, praise, compliments, positive comments—even if it's just, "Well, I will know better next time."

◆ Say kind words to each other in the mirror.

Reporter

Get to know each other, while giving the "interviewee" a chance to talk about herself—almost always a welcomed experience.

DIRECTIONS

Sit down with your child in a comfortable place at a quiet time, maybe at the kitchen table after dinner or on the bed at bedtime. Pretend you're a television reporter. Ask as many of these or similar questions as time and the mood allow:

◇ What is your favorite food? TV show? Game? School subject?

◇ Where is your favorite place to sit in the house (or in the yard)?

◇ Where do you like to go in the town?

◇ What household chore do you prefer or detest?

◇ What makes you happiest or saddest?

◇ Which family pet is most like you?

◇ Which friend would you most confide in?

◇ Whom do you know that reminds you of you?

◇ If you could go anywhere in the world, where would it be?

◇ Do you have a hero or heroine that you admire?

◇ Would you rather be a rock, tree, flower, or cloud?

VARIATIONS

◆ For younger children, choose only one or two questions from the list above. Little ones may not be able to answer these questions for themselves but might easily be able to answer them for their favorite stuffed animal or family pet.

◆ For groups, pair players for the interview, then take turns introducing each other with a simple description, e.g., "This is Joanie and she loves to dance and doesn't mind sweeping. But she'd rather sit beside the flowers in her garden."

◆ Write your answers on separate pieces of paper. For example, everyone writes down the chair in the house he or she most likes to sit in. Shuffle the papers together. One person reads the answers and the others have to guess who said what. One says, "the sofa," and everyone laughs because they know that Dad always likes to lie on the sofa to watch TV or read the paper. It may be a surprise to find out that Idell likes the stool next to the kitchen counter best.

Check It Out

I have played this game with my mother and with my daughters. Each time I was fascinated—sometimes delighted, sometimes surprised—by answers I did not expect. What others value in us can be very different from what we imagine.

DIRECTIONS

Explain to your child that each of you gets to answer your own set of questions on a piece of paper. Afterward, you'll compare your answers.

Your Questions

◇ What is your strongest and best characteristic (the one you feel serves you best in your life)?

◇ What do you think your child thinks is your best characteristic?

◇ What do you think is your child's strongest and best characteristic?

◇ What do you think he or she thinks is best?

◇ What is your best attribute as a parent?

◇ What is your daughter's or son's best attribute as a daughter or son?

◇ What is your weakest characteristic?

◇ What is your child's?

Your Child's Questions

◇ What is your strongest and best characteristic?

◇ What does your mom think is your best?

◇ What is your mother's strongest characteristic?

◇ What do you think she thinks is her strongest?

◇ What is her best attribute as a mother?

◇ What is yours as a daughter or son?

◇ What is your weakest characteristic?

◇ What is your mom's?

Ways to Say "Good"

In Marissa's school, a group of children, ranging in age from five to thirteen, was singing holiday songs with varying degrees of enthusiasm. The older children were unsure that singing was a "cool" thing to do and showed it.

I tried to brighten things up by introducing a song that I had enjoyed as a child. I passed out the photocopies that I had prepared and enthusiastically plunged into the song to show them how it sounded. Unfortunately, my voice squeaked on the highest note. A teenager rolled her eyes.

I felt foolish, but finished anyway.

Later, Marissa came up to me, glowing with pride. "Mom," she said, "you are a hero! You sang a song all by yourself in front of everyone!"

I truly appreciated and needed her comment. There are positive things to say about any situation. Honesty is the best policy, but that may mean talking about what a person has done well instead of what she has not.

DIRECTIONS

The next time your child comes downstairs dressed in a combination of clothes that you never thought would go together (and still do not), try saying in all sincerity, "You certainly have a good imagination!"

Every day for a month, say one of these positive things to your child. Check each off the list as you use it, or add your own statements. See if your child notices the game. If he does, he may enjoy playing it with you, too.

◊ "I like the way you are keeping at your work."

◊ "Thank you very much for this work."

◊ "Wow—I am impressed!"

◊ "That's quite an improvement."

◊ "You certainly have learned a lot about this."

◊ "Congratulations. You got the work done!"

◊ "This really pleases me."

◊ "Exactly right!"

◊ "Now, you've figured it out!"

◊ "That's a very good observation."

◊ "That's coming along very nicely."

◊ "I am very proud of you."

◊ "I appreciate your help."

◊ "I couldn't have done this without you."

◊ "You really taught me something today."

◊ "Very creative."

◊ "Very interesting."

◇ "Marvelous!"

◇ "Perfect."

◇ "Nicely done."

◇ "How impressive."

◇ "You have quite an imagination!"

◇ "Excellent!"

◇ "Superior job!"

◇ "Much better!"

◇ "You're getting it now!"

◇ "That's a good point."

◇ "You're on the right track."

◇ "It looks like you put a lot of work into this."

◇ "I can see a lot of effort in this."

◇ "Good thinking!"

VARIATION

◆ Ask your children what comments from the list they like to hear said to them. Ask if they have other expressions that they like even better.

Positive Spin

Often the very aspect of our character that serves us best is also the aspect that causes us problems.

For example, the person who is very strong-willed may accomplish her goals but may have difficulty getting along with others because she insists on things happening her way.

Consider the person who is very giving and helpful to others. He probably receives a lot of well-deserved love because of it, but may suffer because he never takes time to give to himself—others always come first.

The person who is able to communicate her every thought very well may turn some people on with her lucid words and turn some people off because they feel she talks too much.

DIRECTIONS

Practice putting a positive spin on negative names. See how many words you and your child can add to the following list:

"Fatso" can be "extra rounded"

"Skinny" can be "bare essential"

"Motor mouth" can be "gift for gab"

"Bossy" can be "delegator"

Gotta Have a Dream

As Bloody Mary sang in the musical South Pacific, *"You've got to have a dream. If you don't have a dream, how you gonna make a dream come true?"*

DIRECTIONS

Take turns answering these questions about the future. Open up to all possibilities. After all, you can change your mind tomorrow! Each of you can draw, write, or talk through your answers, depending on which form of expressing yourself is most comfortable.

◇ Where do you want to live? Describe the house and the surroundings—are water, mountains, coastline, forest, a city, or a small town nearby?

◇ Who lives with you? Who lives nearby? Who lives far away?

◇ Describe a typical day. How does it start (feed the pigs, get in a taxi)? What happens next, and then what?

◇ Describe the kind of work you do. Who does it with you?

◇ Where do you go and what do you do on vacations?

VARIATIONS

♦ Try designing for different times in your life. Imagine your life at 15, or 25, or 45, or 85, or all four and tell each other about it, or draw it in a picture.

♦ In a group, each person writes on a slip of paper what he or she wants to be doing in ten years. Put the papers into a hat and pass the hat around. Everyone pulls out a paper. One by one, read each aloud. Together, try to guess whose future it is.

Special Me

This game is fun for family and friends and serves the players twice. Maybe "calm nature" was not the phrase anyone wrote about you, but if someone guessed it was, that's nice, too.

DIRECTIONS

Everyone gets a sheet of paper with everyone else's name on it. If the gathering is large, give each person a paper with just one name on it.

After each name (or the one name), the player writes a compliment, such as "glorious mane of hair" or "calm nature" or "cleanest fingernails" or any other personal quality, however profound or whimsical.

Then, if you used a sheet of paper, cut it into slips. Put the slips into a basket or hat. Each person takes a slip and reads it aloud. Take turns guessing who is being described.

Even Happier

While riding in the car or sitting around the kitchen table, ask your child to think about something she would like to have. Feel free to stretch reality. Her list could include a private spaceship so she can explore the universe or a new eighteen-speed bike to explore the neighborhood.

DIRECTIONS

The job here is to be happy thinking of all the things that might make you even happier. Knowing what you need makes you more likely to get it, or some version of it.

If your child is short on ideas, make a small suggestion. Give her the freedom to completely reject it, consider it, or be deliriously grateful! Sometimes we need someone else to notice what we need to make our lives a little richer.

Chapter 2

ENJOYING MY NAME

There is nothing more precious than the sound of your name. It makes you feel noticed and recognized. In these name games we can hear that lovely sound at least three or four times, and hear people we love saying it.

Names, Names, We All Have Names

CHANT

Names, names, we all have names.

You say yours, we'll say the same.

RESPONSE (Individual)

_____ (name)

RESPONSE (Others)

_____ _____ _____ (name repeated 3 times)

DIRECTIONS

Sit together or facing each other and take turns saying your names. Each time it is your turn, make up a different gesture to accompany your name. like clapping your hands, throwing your arms open, or shaking your head. Everyone repeats the name and gesture three times. Then chant again before the next person takes a turn.

VARIATIONS

♦ Sign your name or make up your own symbol.

♦ Have each player show an attitude while saying their name, for instance, saying it with great pathos or anger.

♦ Say your name in different ways when explaining the game. Saying my name with a breathy Marilyn Monroe voice—Bar-Ba-Ra with my hand behind my head, fluffing my hair—never fails to lighten the moment.

♦ Encourage young children to say their names while clapping out the number of syllables. Jennifer would clap three times. Joe would clap only once.

Names Go Up

This is a good game to play when other children come to visit.

CHANT

> Names go up
> And names go down.
> Tell us how
> your friend's name sounds.

RESPONSE

> _____ (name)

DIRECTIONS

Bring everyone together. Chant this verse using appropriate up and down arm and hand gestures. Players take turns introducing the people next to them.

Who Is This?

CHANT

> Who is this?
> Can anybody tell?
> This is _____ (name)
> And we like (her/him) very well.

DIRECTIONS

In this more advanced game of Peek-a-Boo, cover your face with a scarf. When your child says your name, pull the scarf off and pass it on to him. Now it's his turn to wear the scarf and yours to guess his name.

VARIATION

◆ Instead of using a scarf, you can turn your backs to each other and only turn around when you hear your name.

- ○ 🧍

Who Can Find?

It's nice to get a lot of attention without having to actually do anything. Watch your child's face light up when you find him or her.

CHANT

> Who can find _____(name)?
>
> Who can find _____ (name)?
>
> Who can find _____ (name)?
>
> We want to find (her or him) now!

DIRECTIONS

Chant the questions, naming your child and looking around. Then point to him or her as you chant the last line. Take turns "finding" each other.

- 🧍

Who's Underneath the Hat?

If you happen to have a hat around, here is a variation on the "who can find" theme.

CHANT

> Who's that underneath the hat?
>
> Who can it be?
>
> Who's that underneath the hat?
>
> Let me see!

We've All Got a Name

Young children need practice saying both their first and last names. Adding laughter can make practicing fun.

CHANT

> We've all got a name
> A first and a last.
> Tell us your name and we will laugh.

RESPONSE

_____ _____ (first and last name)

DIRECTIONS

Share a hearty laugh after the response.

VARIATION

♦ Try this chant instead:

> We've all got a name,
> A first and a last.
> Tell us your name and we will clap!

Talking Names

What does your name mean? If you do not have the old baby name book around, it's definitely worth getting a new one. It is so interesting to see what names mean and to learn their country of origin. It is also interesting to know what personal meaning our names secretly hold for us or our families alone.

My younger sister, for instance, was named after her older siblings' adored teenage neighbor who had the coolest card collection in their school. This activity is a good way to share family stories with your child.

DIRECTIONS

Have a conversation with your child about any of these questions:

◊ Do you know how you got your name? If there is a family story about your child's name, this is the time to tell it.

◊ Do you know who chose your name? Was it Mom or Dad, a relative, or friend?

◊ What do you like about your name? Talk about the first, middle, and last names.

◊ What don't you like?

◊ Were you ever teased about your name? If so, talk about how he or she felt about this.

◊ Have you ever heard someone else being teased about their name? Talk about how that person might feel.

◊ Do other people spell your name wrong or mispronounce it? How does that make you feel?

Change Your Name

When I was a young girl, I wanted to be called Babs when I was in a fun-loving mood, Babette when I was in a flirtatious one, and Barbara when I was most grown up. Later I added Baruska to my list to signify the earthy, nature-loving aspect of who I am. I never told anyone. We probably all have many sides to our personality and it might be fun to name them all.

DIRECTIONS

Let imaginations soar. Take turns answering the following questions:

◇ If you could change your name, what would it be and why? Try out new possibilities.

◇ If I could change your name, what would it be? Make up new names for each other, just for fun.

◇ What is your name when you are neat and orderly?

◇ What is your name when you go shopping?

◇ What is your name when you are cooking?

◇ What is your name when you are outdoors hiking?

◇ What is your name when you are your computer self?

PART TWO

Getting to Know Me!

Chapter 3

MY FEELINGS

Our emotions seem so simple. Yet, on the same day, your child may feel mad, goofy, lonely, irritated, anxious, relaxed, impatient, silly, bored, frustrated, jealous, excited, snotty, disgusted, frightened, proud, shy, giddy, guilty, surprised, powerful, relieved, shocked, worried, confident, contented, and disappointed! The following games will let your child explore many emotions.

I've Got a Sound Inside of Me

Here is a good game to play in the late afternoon or evening to help your child express feelings left over from the day's events.

CHANT

_____ (name)
Has a sound inside of (him/her)
That goes like this
(Pause)

RESPONSE

_____ (sound)

DIRECTIONS

Example

The family chants, "Wendy has a sound inside of her that goes like this (pause)." Wendy makes a "yippee" kind of sound because she is pleased. Everyone imitates Wendy's sound two or three times. It is such a powerful and affirming feeling when everybody does what you do!

Next the group chants, "Mom has a sound inside of her that goes like this," and Mom lets out a long sigh because she had a busy day and is just starting to relax. Everyone sighs, too, feeling what Mom feels.

Onward: "Journey has a sound inside of him that goes like this." And Journey, who is still annoyed at something that happen at Little League,

snorts. Because everyone makes the same sound, Journey also feels that he is being heard.

When it is baby Layla's turn, she just sits and looks around. And so does everyone else, enjoying the silence.

Sometimes We're Happy

In this chant, you can change the last word to fit any emotional state. You might want to look at the first paragraph on page 13 for the names of different emotions.

CHANT

Sometimes we're happy.

Sometimes we're sad.

How does _____ (child's name) sound

When (she/he) is _____ (emotion)?

DIRECTIONS

After each chant, the person whose name was called makes the sound that fits the feeling.

VARIATION

♦ Change the chant to:

What does _____ (name) do

When (she/he) is _____ (emotion)?

After each chant, the person whose name is called acts out the emotion. Mention ahead of time that not everyone responds to the same emotion the same way. One person may feel like pounding her fist on a pillow when angry, another might run around the room, and another might want to curl up and turn his back on the world.

How Do You Look?

SONG

(To the tune of "Mary Had a Little Lamb")

> How do you look
>
> When you are mad (or other emotion),
>
> When you are mad,
>
> When you are mad?
>
> How do you look when you are mad?
>
> Won't you show us now?

VARIATIONS

Name an emotion and then:

- ♦ Show how you look with just your face.
- ♦ Show how you look with just your body—face neutral.
- ♦ In the song, change the word "look" to "sound." Show how you sound with each emotion.
- ♦ Change the word "look" to "talk." Say, "It's your turn" or "I want a popsicle" in whatever emotional tone you choose.

The Way You Walk

CHANT

> You can tell how you feel
>
> By the way you walk,
>
> The way you walk,
>
> The way you walk.
>
> Walk, don't talk, right now.

DIRECTIONS

Ask your child to show you how she would walk if she felt a specific emotion. Try to copy your child's exact movements. Then it's your turn. Let her tell you which emotion to "walk." Let her try to copy your exact movements.

Feel So Fine

This game reminds us to notice what things give us pleasure. If we know what they are, we can schedule them into our lives. When your child is older and making her own schedule, she will appreciate this introduction to the habit of penciling in time for her own satisfactions.

CHANT

Won't you tell us, oh friend of mine,

What it is that makes you feel so fine?

DIRECTIONS

Take turns telling each other the special things you like to do.

At the end of the conversation, schedule time to do one of the things that makes your child "feel so fine."

Examples

◇ "You really do love going down slides! How about this Tuesday, after school, we go to the park where the big twirly slide is?"

◇ "That's right, swimming is especially fun for you. Maybe we could make arrangements for you to go with our neighbor to her weekly swim lesson."

◇ "You sure do like being an actress. Do you want to take that box of old clothes down from the attic and put on a play?"

Musical Drawings

One of my happier memories from elementary school is of the time the teacher put on some music and asked us to just draw the way the music made us feel. I stopped feeling bad about my technical skills, which could not compare with the child sitting next to me, who could make a brick house look like a brick house. I was just free to go where the music took me.

DIRECTIONS

Put on some music and join your child in drawing to the music. Give and get the pleasure of letting the music "take you away."

Materials

Paper and pencils or markers, or paints and paint brush, music recordings

Movin' and Groovin'

DIRECTIONS

Put on one type of music you enjoy. Listen to it with your child, and as you feel it, move around together to express the feeling the music gives you. Then change to another type of music and repeat the experience.

VARIATION

♦ Make a tape using a few minutes from several different types of songs. One at a time, take turns moving to that song and copying each other's movements. You can replay the tape many times and see how each of you differently expresses a range of feelings to the same songs.

Materials

Country, jazz, rock, classical, folk or ethnic music recordings

Laugh Till You Cry, Cry Till You Laugh

Go back and forth with your child, or around in a circle if you are in a group. You do not really need a large group to play; you only need to pay attention to each other.

DIRECTIONS

Start with a smile. Your child or the next person adds on a bigger smile, the next person a giggle, the next a short laugh. The next person adds a big guffaw, the next a long belly laugh, the next an almost hysterical laugh session. The next turns it into a sobbing session, and the next into crying. The next turns the crying into sniffling, the next into a frown that turns into a sad smile. The next offers a little smile, and the next a bigger smile.

VARIATION

♦ Each person may want to do the whole gamut, slowly building up the emotions until the switch is made from laughter to sadness or vice-versa.

Silent Stories

This is a simple game of moving with feelings without using words.

DIRECTIONS

Choose one or more of the scenarios below to act out without words. Take turns with your child. Play yourself. It is okay to elaborate on the story as much as you would like to bring out the main emotion.

◇ Anger: You just got blamed for something your brother did and your dad will not listen to your side of the story. Your dad is walking away from you, and you are following him.

◇ Fear: It's very late at night and very dark. You swear you just heard a scratching sound in your closet, and the closet door is open. You have to go past it to go to the bathroom, and you really have to go.

◇ Joy: Your parents just told you they are taking you to Disneyland, but first they are going to stop at the toy store where you can pick out anything you want. Move with those feelings as if you were walking to get into the car.

◇ Embarrassment: The teacher just called on you to come to the front of the room and answer the question and you realize you were not paying attention. You do not have any idea what she is talking about, and all the other kids seem to understand perfectly. You are expected to walk up to the front of the room. Show us how you would walk.

◇ Love: This morning, your mom, for no apparent reason, has just put her arms around you and her face next to yours. She has told you how special and wonderful you are, how happy she has been to have you in her life, and how proud she is of you. You are now walking out the door to go to school.

Cross the Line

DIRECTIONS

Determine or draw a line on the floor or the ground. Take turns walking to the line as if you were feeling one of the emotions below, and when you cross the line, switch into another emotion. Use your whole body—head, shoulders, back, hands, and feet.

◇ Brave turning to fearful

◇ Proud turning to humble

◇ Joyful turning to despairing

◇ Angry turning to calm

◇ Serious turning to silly

Body Talk

DIRECTIONS

Take turns making shapes with your bodies that say:

◇ No!   ◇ Yes!

◇ Here I am.   ◇ I am grumpy.

◇ I am shy.   ◇ I am so tired.

◇ Leave me alone.   ◇ Never!

◇ Don't mess with me.

VARIATIONS

◆ Make the shape using just shoulders, neck, and back.

◆ Convey the words just by clapping.

Faces Have Feelings

DIRECTIONS

Take turns showing how you look experiencing one of the emotions listed below. Guess which emotion is being expressed.

- ◇ Hungry
- ◇ Mad
- ◇ Scared
- ◇ Lazy
- ◇ Bored
- ◇ Picked on
- ◇ Gloomy
- ◇ Cool
- ◇ Motherly
- ◇ Goofy
- ◇ Proud
- ◇ Guilty
- ◇ Disgusted
- ◇ Anxious
- ◇ Weird
- ◇ Ashamed
- ◇ Joyful

VARIATION

- ◆ Write these emotions on pieces of paper, put them in a hat or bowl, and take turns picking one to demonstrate.

Same Words, Different Voice

DIRECTIONS

Say the same expression with different feelings. Say, for example, "Don't do it" with anger, then with sadness, then with fear, and then flirtatiously. Try it. They are very different, aren't they?

Here are other expressions to try. Say them each in four ways—with anger, sadness, fear, and flirtation:

◇ I am going home.

◇ Do it now.

◇ Here I am.

◇ Watch out.

VARIATION

♦ Try saying the same expressions in other ways, such as questioning, bored, surprised, and happy.

Act It Out

Have you noticed how you use your whole body to express your emotions? Maybe you are limp when you're sad, get stiff when you're angry. Perhaps you feel expanded when you're happy and contracted when afraid.

DIRECTIONS

Take turns acting out the way these statements make you feel. This time, try using words along with your gestures.

◇ Your dog died.

◇ Everyone was invited to the party but you.

◇ You won the lottery.

◇ A bear is chasing you.

◇ Your best friend and you are going on a great adventure.

◇ You have to give a speech in front of the whole school.

◇ You're at a new place and don't know anyone.

◇ You're on a white-water rafting trip and you can't swim.

◇ You're canoeing a beautiful lake and you're loving it.

◇ You're 90 cents short of the money you need to buy something you really want at the store.

◇ You found a million dollars.

◇ Everyone went to the movies but you.

◇ You have to go to a new school or start a new job.

VARIATION

♦ Express these same emotions with just hands or arms or eyes or mouth or fingers or any other single body part.

The Shadow Side

Even children can have temporary irritable moods that last for several days and make them hard to live with. During those times, if children can recognize their bad moods and have an outlet for their irritable feelings, they may be less liable to inflict their crankiness on others.

My husband knows a lot about cranky moods. As he puts it, "I always wanted to live with beautiful women. When I got my wish, I found that I also had to live with the emotional swings of pregnancies, puberties, and many, many periods. And just when I thought I was finished, along came menopause!"

DIRECTIONS

Show your child how to air his complaints to his shadow side. Set up a light that shines on a wall. Invite him to stand in front of the light, casting his shadow onto the wall. Then he can tell his shadow all his troubles.

If your child wants you to listen, stay for the conversation, or, if he prefers, leave him alone with his shadow friend.

How Mad Are You?

One day Marissa and I were on an easy Class 1 canoe trip. Even though I had canoed in much trickier Class 3-plus white water before, I found myself nervously raising my voice and yelling out "Pry, Pry!" at every teeny bump.

Finally, Marissa turned to me and said, "Mom, you're having a Class 3 fear on a Class 1 run!"

We had a good laugh. Ever since, we use that measure as our code to signal when either one of us feels that the other is overreacting.

DIRECTIONS

Someday, when your emotions are not in high gear, work out a code with your child.

For instance, if you assigned a number to the feeling you called sadness, what would cause a number one, low level of sadness? What about a number five or ten? For me, a number one, low-level sadness would be rain on a day I had hoped to garden. A number five might be if my computer lost something I had spent an hour writing, and a ten would be if someone got seriously hurt or died.

Codes make it easier to describe feelings. You might ask, "How much do you want to do this between one and ten?" If the answer is seven, then you might try harder to make it happen than if the answer were four.

VARIATION

◆ Codes do not have to be numbers. They can be movements. You might say to your young child, "How big is your sadness? Show me with your hands. If your hands are close together, you are only a tiny bit sad. If they are far apart, you are sad big time."

Show Me a Ten

Each person has his or her own level of intensity for expressing an emotion; there is no right or wrong level. Your level is all you need to know to understand yourself, even though it is good to know that many levels are possible for other people.

DIRECTIONS

Try acting out and exaggerating the emotions listed in Faces Have Feelings (see page 52). Make your movements bigger, and then even bigger. Then make them smaller, and then so small that your feelings may only be apparent from the way you hold your mouth or a look in your eye.

Give your movements code numbers. An exaggerated movement is a ten; a subtle one is a one. Then you can play the game by saying, "Show me a ten ashamed; now do a three joyful."

Should or Could Door

Having options makes life more enjoyable. The next time your child is facing a tough task, try making a game of creating options.

DIRECTIONS

Pretend there are two doors to open. The first is the "Should" door and the second the "Could" door. Pretend to open the first door and walk through, saying, for instance, "I *should* do my homework." Then pretend to open the second door and walk through, saying, "I *could* get my math and English done now, and then I could call my girlfriend and do my geometry with her." Show your child it's more fun to go through the "Could" door. Then have him try it, filling in his particular choices.

Examples

◇ I *should* do the dishes now.

I *could* put some good music on and then do the dishes.

◇ I *should* clean my room now.

I *could* go to the park today because it is so beautiful out and clean my room when I get back.

Envious and Annoyed

The things that annoy us about others could be traits we do not like in ourselves. The things that we envy in others are often our own unrealized potentials. Children commonly have difficulty recognizing these feelings. You can show your child how.

DIRECTIONS

Does your child envy or feel annoyed by someone? Together, list that person's traits. Discuss the funny way in which they might actually be seen as positive qualities a really nice person might want to possess. Finally, brainstorm together a list of activities that would help your child achieve those potentials.

Materials

Pencil and paper

Examples

◇ The person I envy is a leader and everyone wants to do what she does. I have a tendency to be bossy, too—maybe that is the leader in me wanting to come out. I could find a group that would like me to lead.

Possibilities

Run a playgroup for the little kids in the neighborhood once a week.

Take turns having an "I am in charge" day with friends or family.

Get a puppy.

◇ The person who annoys me is so needy and whiny. Maybe that bothers me because I never ask for help when I need it and really want someone to help me. Perhaps I could work on asking for help a little more often.

Possibilities

Be aware of when I want attention and notice how I get what I need.

Praise myself for times when I meet my own needs.

Hang out with a cat, an animal that can be independent but also knows how to ask for attention.

What's Not Wrong

Life is a continual process of savoring the "ups" and working out of the "downs." It takes practice to appreciate rainy days as much as days when the sun is shining. As a friend of mine said, be thankful for every day, and "cultivate the attitude of gratitude." Nothing is too small to recognize as something that is not *wrong!*

DIRECTIONS

Take turns naming something that is "not wrong," such as:

"None of my teeth hurt."

"My heart feels light today."

"I had a good lunch."

"My brother didn't hit me."

"I got to be first at the water fountain."

Calendar Game

When my family and I moved, we experienced a difficult period of adjustment before we found the right house, made friends, figured out what to buy at the grocery store, and felt at home again. This activity helped us not be too discouraged.

DIRECTIONS

At each day's end, write down just one thing that happened that made you happy. It could be the smallest incident like a friendly moment with a neighbor's dog or a smile and kind look from a stranger. It could be a delicious swim in the lagoon or the warmth of the sun on your skin. Anything good counts. Before long, you may notice too many good things to be able to write them all down anymore. Have family members keep their own calendars. Share them from time to time.

Materials

Calendars or notebooks

Nighttime List

DIRECTIONS

After you have read your young child the usual bedtime story, tell her the story of her day, mentioning all the good things that happened.

Example

There was a lovely little boy named Josh who woke up in the morning and ate pancakes with yogurt and maple syrup on top—his favorite breakfast. Then he went with his mother and his doggie, Daisy, to the park and played on the slide and the swings. Later, he saw his good friend Melanie and they had fun splashing in the pool together until Josh fell down. But then he stopped hurting and had some fun making sailboats out of leaves and making them go. Then Josh and his mommy and Daisy had a picnic lunch by the pond before coming home for nap time. After nap, they went to the grocery store and Josh got to pick out the cereal he liked best. At last, Josh, tired from his big day, kissed his mommy goodnight and went fast asleep.

The Body Knows

This game gives a vacation to the part of your brain that says That's a dumb idea or How could you feel that way? Listen to what your body says instead.

DIRECTIONS

Schedule some quiet time together to find out what your bodies know. Clear a space, move furniture if needed, and just move the way you feel like moving. Do not put on any music. Just move freely to your mood.

Attitude Adjustments

Practice putting a positive spin on any situation. As Thomas Edison said, "I have not failed 10,000 times. I have successfully found 10,000 things that did not work!"

DIRECTIONS

Give your child practice in seeing the bright side of life. Take turns imagining positive outcomes to negative experiences. Use the examples below or feel free to make up other scenes.

◇ Your friends get invited to a party, but you don't.

Possibilities

> You end up doing something else you like a whole lot better with someone you love and who really loves you.

> You decide that maybe these are not your true friends and you find people who are better friends.

> You realize that you have been especially negative to your friends and hurting their feelings. Maybe this experience is a "wake-up call" for you to change your behavior.

◇ It rains the day you planned to go to the zoo.

Possibilities

> You go anyway with a fun pal and a big umbrella. You have the place to yourself and see other animals who enjoy the rain.

> You end up staying home and playing a dynamite game of Monopoly.

> You put on your slicker and big rain boots, splash in every puddle you find, and look closely at the earthworms.

Now you come up with possibilities

◇ You have to deal with the kid who always cuts into the line ahead of you.

◇ Your supposed "best friend" chose a new "best friend."

◇ Your family is moving to a new town where you don't know anyone.

◇ You were in a recital and made a mistake.

◇ People laughed at you when you misunderstood a slang word or expression because English is not your first language.

Admiration Game

When I am admiring my cat and noticing how beautiful her coat is, how soft her fur feels, how magnificent her green eyes look, how sweet her breath smells, I cannot help feeling fine. It's true—one good thought usually leads to another! This is a very good activity to do when your child is having a hard time.

Materials

Clock or watch with a second hand, mirror (optional)

DIRECTIONS

Take turns admiring something aloud. You go first. Ask your child to time how long you can focus on the object and keep talking. The rule of the game is that you must keep noticing admirable things for 20 seconds. Then invite your child to try the game.

Example

If you chose a flower that pleases you, notice and say how nicely the petals arrange themselves, the pretty color of the stamen, the feel of the stem, the fragrance, the shading.

After 20 seconds, notice how your thoughts extend beyond the object itself, perhaps to a lovely garden you saw long ago. Describe that, too.

VARIATIONS

♦ Do an admiration focus on each other for at least 20 seconds. The "admiree" has to be quiet and take it in.

♦ In front of a mirror, play this game, focusing on yourselves.

Name It

We have many emotions in the course of a day. Some are fleeting; some are undercurrents. Some are impossible to ignore and others are almost too subtle to notice.

It is helpful for children to be able to recognize and name an emotion. They are less likely to act inappropriately if they really know what they are feeling. Even when my children were little, I would ask them, "How do you feel about that?" partly because I was curious to know what little kids felt about things and partly to increase their awareness of their own feelings.

At one point in their late adolescence, a friend of theirs began to tease me about my habit, "How do you fe-el about that?" she would mock. My daughters would join her.

But now that they are young adults, I can see they all agree with me. I never have to ask my children or their friends how they feel. It's just part of our regular conversations.

DIRECTIONS

Be a model for your child of a person who is aware of her feelings. It is not necessary to do anything with the emotions. It is enough simply to let your child see how to take a moment to recognize the feelings.
In your everyday conversation, include feeling phrases, such as:

"I am feeling sad this morning, so I think I will take a walk."

"When that happens, I feel angry."

"Writing letters is frustrating for me."

"I just feel like singing today!"

"I feel anxious today, and I am not sure why."

VARIATIONS

♦ You might just want to say, "Hello, sadness. I feel you and recognize you and will let you go through me for a while." In this way, your child sees that an emotion does not need to get very big or last very long to get your attention.

♦ Every day, perhaps at a different time each day, remember to ask how your child feels. When you take the time to ask children how they feel, they learn that these emotions have names and that you care.

Chapter 4

MY REACTIONS

Our reactions are important guides to what we want and what we don't want. Children need to know how they react to lots of things—and that their reactions matter. We help them learn this when we take the time to check in on their feelings. It's also a way of letting them know that they themselves are important to us. These games will give you lots of practice in "checking in" and your child lots of reactions to consider.

How Much Space Do You Need Today?

We all have a space around ourselves that is our own. Usually we get physically uncomfortable when people get inside our space without an implicit or explicit invitation. This activity lets children discover their space.

I used to be under the impression that the size of one's space is a static thing. Then, one day I was doing this activity with my daughter and her boyfriend. She had just come from a stressful day and began to feel some discomfort when we were still quite far away.

We all laughed and realized that personal space is actually an active thing that grows and shrinks. Many factors influence it, such as mood, attitude, self-image, and certainly your feeling about the person coming toward you.

DIRECTIONS

One person stands still. A second person stands about 10 feet away. Taking a step at a time, the second person begins to walk toward the other, asking with each step, "Is this still comfortable?" When the first person begins to feel some change, such as a slight feeling of anxiousness or skin just beginning to feel creepy, she or he says, "Stop."

Try playing this activity at different times to see how much or how little your personal space changes with different moods.

What Comes Up?

DIRECTIONS

Call out one of the following words.

School, lotion, alarm clock, television, camera, heater, homework, kitten, hurricane, telephone, snow, diamond, glue, dentist, gynecologist, shoe clerk, machinist, fortune teller, policeman, robbery, mugging, figure skater, auto accident, stuck elevator, ocean, fallen tree, kitchen, bed, cuddling, arguing, kissing.

Feel free to add others or make up your own. Encourage your players to make whatever facial expression or movement the word evokes. Is it positive, negative, neutral?

Get What You Want

We each have different ways of dealing with different people. Your child knows that whining sometimes works with Mom but will definitely not work with older brother. Children are sensible, and as the bumper sticker said, "Insanity is doing the same thing over and over and expecting different results."

Here's a way to help your child get positive reactions more often. Awareness always precedes change, so this activity encourages self-awareness.

DIRECTIONS

Without speaking, go up to another person and try to take something—such as the person's chair or an article of clothing.

See what methods work with various personalities—gesturing politely, whining, pouting, flirting—and reward the kind of behavior you want to encourage.

VARIATIONS

♦ Let one player walk across the room. The other player tries to stop her from reaching the end. How does the stopped player react? Give up? Elicit help? Be forceful, tricky, or evasive?

♦ See if using words changes the dynamics, and if so, how.

♦ One player tries to get another to come with him. Try different methods. See which one works.

Expectations

Life is unpredictable but sometimes it helps to imagine it just the way you'd like it.

One time Roxanne was worried about losing a friend she had made. She acted out a phone conversation she wished they would have. She took both parts. Afterwards she felt hopeful that things might work out and was less worried.

An hour later her friend called and they had almost that exact conversation because she was clear about how she felt and what she wanted to say.

DIRECTIONS

When your child is worried about an event that happened or will happen, ask her to imagine what is the best thing that could happen next or the way she would like it to be. It helps sort things out.

VARIATION

♦ Before going on an outing or vacation, or at the start of each day, describe to each other how you'd like it to go. Enjoy the description. Even if it doesn't turn out the way you imagined, at least you had a good time thinking about it.

Materials

None or pen and paper or tape recorder

Some of Your Favorite Things

The first time I played this game, I was surprised. I thought of myself as a "people person" who loved parties and social events. I found that higher on my list of enjoyable activities were playing the piano and other solitary activities. So I began to make more time for those things, much to my great satisfaction.

For example, when I was little and supposed to be practicing "Papa Hayden" and other beginning songs on the piano, I loved to make wonderful sounds of thunder and lightning. I would run my hand down the keyboard to simulate rain. My mom used to yell down, "Stop that banging!" but it was music to me. Now I have my own piano and make all the made-up music I want.

DIRECTIONS

Make a list of at least ten things you enjoy doing—including little things such as folding clothes, doodling, daydreaming, and whistling. Help your child do the same. Put the lists in sight, maybe on the refrigerator. The next time one of you is feeling out of sorts, check to see if you have been doing enough of the things on your list.

VARIATION

♦ Ask each other questions about the items on your lists to see if there is a theme:

"Do these interests cost money?"

"Are these things to do with others or alone?"

"Are these mostly indoors or outdoors?"

"Do I have the education to do these now or do I need more information?"

"Are these long-time interests or are these new?"

"Do I do any of these things regularly?"

Listening

We all have a clear inner voice that we can hear if we are very still, as I was reminded when a friend told me this story:

Once there was a woman who lost her diamond ring in a pool. She kept diving and jumping around frantically in the pool trying to find it, but to no avail. A friend suggested that instead she sit quietly beside the water and see what happened. She did and the water became calm and clear and the ring shone and became apparent.

As we increase our capacity to hear ourselves, we increase our understanding of our needs. Listening becomes a way of "checking in."

DIRECTIONS

Sit still with your child. Get away from the phone and other possible interruptions, just for a while. Sit quietly and be totally there, ready to listen, even to the silence.

VARIATIONS

♦ If your child is troubled, suggest, "Why don't you just sit with this for a while before you decide what to do" or "Maybe you should sleep on it."

♦ If your child asks you for advice, say "I feel many ways about it. Let's just think on it for a while." Take a moment to listen to your inner voice before you respond. Ask your child to listen to his.

Group Freeze

Some people do best if they are in the center of things, others prefer to be more on the edges, and some like a little of both. There is no place that is better than another; it's just nice to know what you like.

DIRECTIONS

Everyone walks around a big, empty space. After a while, call out "Freeze." Ask all the participants to note where they are in relation to the group. Are they on the inside, nearer the outer edge, or somewhere in between?

Ask each child if this position in the group is where he or she usually likes to be.

Earth, Air, Fire, Water

In this game a person's style is likened to one of the basic elements.
*   Some people hold their ground and cannot be moved (earth).*
*   Others forge ahead and make things happen their way (fire).*
*   Some just get out of the way and cannot be confronted (air).*
*   Others appear to yield and find a way around the situation to get what*
they need (water).

DIRECTIONS

Players experiment with these styles by walking around in the ways listed below. After they have experienced each posture, ask, "Which, if any, feels most like you?" (If you are not sure which position is most "you," you might check the soles of your shoes and see where they are most worn.)

◇ Fire: Weight is toward the front of the feet and the outsides of the feet. Chest is forward. As players walk around in this bold position, have them say aloud or to themselves the words "I see it and do it."

◇ Water: Weight is on the heels and insides of the feet. Pelvis is forward. The words are serene. "I yield and then I act."

◇ Air: Weight is on the heels and outsides of the feet, leaning back slightly. The words are spacey. "I don't resist. I get out of the way."

◇ Earth: Weight is forward and on the insides of the feet. The words are firm: "I am here. I am not being moved."

VARIATIONS

♦ Players work in pairs. Each person takes a different posture and moves toward the partner. What does it feel like to be in a Fire walk and approach someone who is in an Earth mode? How does a person being Air react to a person being Water?

♦ Line up two rows of players facing each other and have them walk toward each other and around each other while in different modes.

Chapter 5

MY SENSES

Information about the external world comes in through our vision, hearing, taste, smell, touch, and intuition (our sixth sense). Children who are oblivious to this stream of information are missing out on some important data. Without realizing why, they feel less able to cope with the world.

We can help the children in our lives develop well-honed information-gathering tools by playing games that increase sensory awareness.

The Feeling Walk

DIRECTIONS

Take a walk together—along a country lane or on a sidewalk. Say that for the next few moments you want to be very aware of how things feel. While you are walking, say:

◇ Notice your feet walking on the surface of the earth, even if it's paved. Can you feel your feet connecting with the surface?

◇ Now, feel the air on your skin. Stop and turn slowly around in a circle. Is the wind blowing any harder from any one direction? Is it damp or dry?

◇ Now, just listen to sounds. Listen for the sounds underneath the other sounds, including the sound of air going in your nose.

◇ Can you combine senses—like feeling the air on your skin and listening to a specific sound at the same time?

◇ What do you see? Look for things that you have not noticed before.

◇ Now feel your body. Is your spine straight? Are your head and neck relaxed? This is a good time to practice walking with your body in alignment.

VARIATIONS

♦ Do the same game while sitting comfortably at home. Have your child sit with eyes closed and ask these questions:

♦ How are you feeling? Relaxed? Tense? Sleepy? Excited?

♦ What sounds do you hear? Name them.

♦ What smells do you smell?

♦ How are you breathing? Fast, slow, shallow, deep?

♦ How do your clothes feel on your body? Comfortable? Itchy? Warm?

♦ Do you have any taste in your mouth from something recently eaten?

♦ How does the air feel around you? Warm? Cool? Dry? Moist?

Hide and Seek

DIRECTIONS

While playing Hide and Seek with your young child, give auditory clues to where you are hiding, that is, make noises from your hiding places. Start with quiet sounds.

Background Sounds

DIRECTIONS

Ask your child to be very quiet, then tell you all the sounds he starts to hear, such as:

The tick of a clock, distant traffic, birds chirping, fan blowing, wind.

Imagine Sounds

DIRECTIONS

Ask your child to be very quiet, then take turns naming sounds that you imagine, such as:

Creaking of an old house, dashing of waves on huge rocks, lapping of water on the shore, a fire siren far away, frying bacon sizzling, ice cubes crackling in warm water.

Who's Talking?

DIRECTIONS

One person turns her back to the family or group. You point to someone in the group who just starts to talk. He can say anything, from a greeting to a line from a poem such as "Baa Baa Black Sheep" in his own voice or disguising it with an accent. The person with her back turned has to say whose voice it is.

What's Talking?

DIRECTIONS

Put a blindfold over your child's eyes, a paper bag on her head, or ask her to turn her back to you. You go around the room knocking on or manipulating different things, while she gets to guess what is being knocked on or used.

You can ask a younger child to identify a more common sound like the opening of the refrigerator. You can ask an older child to identify a more subtle sound, such as tapping on a window pane.

Take turns being the noisemaker and the listener.

VARIATIONS

◆ Use different body sounds: hand slapping knee, feet stomping, fingers snapping, tongue clicking, and so on. Ask your child to guess how you are making the noise.

◆ Use different objects in the room and have the objects identified by the sound they make when falling. (Best not to use this version with really young kids, or you may be identifying the sound of glass breaking!)

Whispers

A teacher I know uses this game to excuse students to go wash their hands before lunch. She whispers each name. The children are so eager to be excused that the whole class is very, very quiet, listening to be whisperingly called.

If you want a group to be quiet, whispering works better than yelling, because everyone wants to hear what it is they are not supposed to hear.

DIRECTIONS

Whisper the name of any person in your group very, very softly. When the person hears his name, he jumps up (or raises a hand, stands up, or salutes).

If the players do not hear their names, increase the volume slightly until they do.

Clap the Same

DIRECTIONS

One person claps a simple beat or a certain number of claps and the others imitate that clap.

Witch and Cat

DIRECTIONS

All the players except one sit on the floor in a half circle. They are the cats. The one standing is the witch. She goes a short distance from the cats and stands with her back to them. When one of the cats meows, the witch turns around and tries to guess which cat it was. If she guesses correctly, she gets another turn (You might want to make two turns the maximum so everyone gets a chance.) If the witch guesses incorrectly, the cat that meowed takes a turn as the witch.

Popcorn

DIRECTIONS

The children squat, pretending they are kernels of corn waiting until they hear the number 10. You start counting 1, 2, 3, 4. . . . At 10 they go off, going from a squat to a full jump and then jump all around, forward and backward until you start a new batch of popcorn. If you're in a silly mood, eat them all up.

VARIATION

♦ Give different kids different numbers to pop at. Some start popping at 4, some at 6. Remind them to listen for their numbers.

Spaceship

DIRECTIONS

Everyone is a spaceship, squatting. Count down 10, 9, 8, 7, 6, and so on, until it's time to BLAST OFF!

Everyone counts backward together and blasts off together, roaring and jumping.

Moving Colors

DIRECTIONS

Name four or more colors and show the players how to move to each color. As you call out the different colors, the players do the corresponding movement. Keep varying the amount of time they have between color changes so they have to think fast and listen well and cannot anticipate your direction.

Example

When you say "green," the players should sway back and forth like tall blades of grass.

When you say "red," players should hop on one foot as if they just burned it.

When you say "blue," players should flap their arms and fly like a blue-bird.

When you say "yellow," players should spin like a top.

VARIATIONS

♦ Use sounds instead of colors. For example, a hum means to skip; a whistle means to walk backwards; a leg slap means to jump.

♦ If you have a larger group, assign some to be the "sound makers." The leader can stand behind the sound makers and touch the back of the one that should make the next sound. Whenever the sound is made, the rest of the kids move accordingly.

The leader has the possibility of moving the game along at various speeds and in varying order, making it all wonderfully unpredictable.

Hum a Song

If you are traveling or stuck in traffic and have a strong need to make the moment more pleasant, try playing this game with your child.

DIRECTIONS

Players take turns humming a song and identifying the name of the song.

Silly Sentences

Sometimes, when I am talking to my children and have a strong suspicion they are not really listening, I slip in the words, "peanut butter and jelly" to see if they notice. They are aware of my trick now, but it still works. It alerts them to tune back in if their thoughts have strayed. And if they do not notice, it alerts me that I am not capturing their attention.

DIRECTIONS

Say a group of sentences, most of which make perfectly good sense. Insert one sentence that does not, and see who is listening.

Examples

◇ I eat with my mouth. I feel with my hands. I jump with my feet. I hop with my tongue. I touch with my hands. I run with my legs.

◇ I get up in the morning, go to the bathroom, brush my teeth, put on my pajamas, go eat breakfast, and go to school.

◇ I take the bread out of the sink, put it in the toaster, butter it, and eat it up.

What Doesn't Fit?

DIRECTIONS

Say a group of words that are in the same category, except for one that does not fit. When players hear that word, they make an appropriate sound, such as BUZZZZ.

Examples

◇ Milk, eggs, meat, lotion, butter, sauce

◇ Cat, rabbit, ear, elephant, kangaroo

◇ Chair, table, pillow, tree, stool

◇ Worrying, laughing, snoring, crying, giggling

◇ Gum, celery, cotton candy, gumdrops, chocolate

Remember

DIRECTIONS

Read a list of related words to your child. Maybe it's a list of animals or a group of words that begin with the letter B. He listens to the list and then tries to repeat it. Then it's his turn to make a list for you to repeat.

Hummingbird

DIRECTIONS

One player leaves the room and the group decides where to hide a small object somewhere in the room. When the player returns, she tries to find the object. When she is near the object, the other players hum loudly, and when far from it, softly.

VARIATIONS

♦ The players are sitting in a circle and one sits on the object, such as a penny. The searching player walks up to each player while the others hum loudly or softly.

♦ When the object is found, the player who was sitting on the penny leaves the room and becomes the next "searching player."

♦ Instead of hiding an object, hide a person.

♦ Instead of humming, use breath. Breathe loudly when the player is close to the object or person, breathe quietly when not. The listener will really have to pay attention.

Sound Seekers

DIRECTIONS

Players make different sounds with their bodies. Possibilities: Snap fingers, clap hands, slap knees, stomp feet, smack lips. Another player is brought blindfolded into the group and has to find a certain sound, say finger snapping. The seeker wanders among the sound makers until the one making the identified sound is found.

Tell a Story

If you have mixed skill levels in your group, assign appropriately simple or complex words or sounds to different people.

DIRECTIONS

Tell a story to the players with the stipulation that whenever you say a certain word they have to make a specified noise like clap hands, hiss, or snap fingers. The word could be common, like "and," or one that appears infrequently in the story.

The word could also be any animal, any form of transportation, anything made of metal, or anything that ends with a certain letter.

Numbers

DIRECTIONS

This game requires six or more people to work well. The group forms a circle with "It" in the middle. Each person in the circle has a number from one to however many people are in the group. "It" calls out two numbers, say, four and eight. The children whose numbers are four and eight try to change position by running to each other's spots in the circle while "It" tries to get in one of their places. The more spread out the circle is, the bigger the challenge. Adjust the size to fit the group's needs.

Opposites

Everyone knows Simon Says, right? That's a game in which the leader gives commands and everyone follows instructions. This game works a little differently. You give a command and everyone else is supposed to do the opposite, or at least something quite different from what you ask.

DIRECTIONS

Stand facing your child. Explain the game and see what happens when you give the following commands. Accompany your command with the appropriate gestures. Remember, your player is supposed to do the opposite of what you say and do!

◇ Walk forward

◇ Walk backward

◇ Put your hands on your head

◇ Put your hands on your feet

◇ Look down

◇ Look up

◇ Go to your right

◇ Go to your left

◇ Touch your toe

◇ Put your hands in front of you

◇ Put your hands in back of you

◇ Sit down

◇ Stand up

◇ Cross your arms

◇ Stretch out your arms

VARIATIONS

◆ For older children, mix up the above orders so they are not in such a logical sequence. The children will have to listen even harder.

◆ For younger children, start by having them do what you say. Later, switch to having them do the opposite.

Bat Gang

DIRECTIONS

In a large uncluttered space, blindfold the players. Have them find each other by making noises, as if they were the humming of a bat's radar. Every time they find one another, they can make a squeal (which seems to happen naturally anyway) and then join together in looking for others until all the players form a huge blob.

VARIATION

♦ Only one person is blindfolded. The others make noises to indicate their positions.

   This is the land version of the pool game Marco Polo. The seeker says "Marco" and the others respond "Polo" to identify their positions. Decide ahead of time if the other players can keep moving around or need to remain still until found.

Freeze Run

This game is a good excuse to run around wildly with no particular reason except to release energy.

DIRECTIONS

Everyone runs (or hops, dances, skips backward, or jumps) until you say "Freeze." Encourage everyone to stop instantly. They have to hold that frozen position until you say "Thaw."

VARIATION

♦ Instead of saying words, make sounds—one for "Freeze" and another for "Thaw." To raise the level of difficulty of play, make the sound more softly.

Do What I Say, Not What I Do

This game requires the players to really listen and not be confused by what they see, and leaders to stay alert and not get mixed up.

DIRECTIONS

Tell your group to line up next to each other. When everyone is in place, tell them to do what you say and not what you do, then give directions to each individual, one at a time. A player who follows directions correctly takes a step forward. A player who doesn't follow directions takes a step backward.

Whoever makes it across the room first gets to be leader next.

Example

Touch your mouth and say, "Sara, touch your nose," or jump and say, "Eddie, stamp your foot."

Sleeping Miser

DIRECTIONS

One person is the miser and pretends to be sleeping at one end of the room. The others are thieves who want to sneak up and steal the miser's treasure lying nearby. The miser has his eyes closed. When he hears someone getting close, he points to that person, with his eyes still closed. If he is pointing in the right direction, that "thief" has to go back to the other end of the room. If he does not, the thieves keep sneaking up until someone is quiet and sneaky enough to steal the treasure. The successful thief becomes the next miser.

Do This, Do That

This is another variation of the classic Simon Says.

DIRECTIONS

No one is supposed to move unless the leader says "Do this."

The leader stands on one leg (or any other action) and says, "Do this." Everyone imitates the leader's action. Then the leader quickly does something else, like jump up, and says, "Do that." Of course, as you remember, no one is supposed to move. And of course, someone will!

Anyone who moves on "Do that" more than three times is out of the game.

VARIATION

♦ Choose other kinds of consequences for moving on "Do that," such as helping make snacks for everyone still in the game.

Sound Orchestra

DIRECTIONS

The children are the sound orchestra. Each chooses a sound to make. Possibilities include:

Animal sounds, car or train sounds, crying or laughing, tongues clicking, lips flapping, whistling, or a made-up, nonsense sound.

Take turns being the conductor, pointing a "baton" (or finger) to indicate who or what group gets to make their sound. The conductor can indicate with hand gestures which sounds she wants to be loud or soft, drawn-out or staccato. She can also intersperse various solos, duos, or trios, or let the entire orchestra play together.

Everyone gets a chance to be the conductor, the one who gets to compose the "music."

Nonsense Walk

This game combines good listening and movement. It helps to have a leader who is quick about making up nonsense words. Even if only two people play, you'll still have fun!

DIRECTIONS

The players line up, side by side, and face the leader. The leader takes four steps forward while saying "Ish ki bibble, ish ki bu" in 4/4 time in the singsong cadence drill sergeants use.

Listening simultaneously, the players take 4 steps back. Then they take 4 steps forward, repeating the "words." While the players are stepping forward speaking, the leader takes 4 steps backward listening.

The leader steps forward again in 4/4 time, saying, "Hallo bu bit, be nonka tu." The group walks their 4 steps backward while these words are said, then takes four steps forward repeating them.

When the group can move forward or backward with the words in the right place, make up hand gestures to go along with the words.

What's Inside, What's Outside?

DIRECTIONS

Give your child a certain amount of time (the older, the longer) to just look out the window and see all the things there are to see outside. She can list them on a piece of paper or call them out. Then notice all the things that are inside and list them, too.

Materials
Pencil and paper

Mind's Eye

DIRECTIONS

Read the following list aloud very, very slowly. Ask the players to try to see each image in their minds.

◇ A wrinkled, old face

◇ A snow-covered field

◇ Faraway mountains

◇ An underground cave

◇ A castle in the sky

◇ A road winding through the hills

◇ Cotton candy

VARIATION

◆ Have the players make up different images for others to "see."

Look at Me

DIRECTIONS

Stare at each other for a minute. Then close your eyes or turn your backs and list as many visual details as you can about the other person.

What's Different?

DIRECTIONS

Let your child, the observer, look at you for a moment. Tell him to notice where you are sitting, in what position, and what you are wearing. Then ask him to leave the room.

While he is gone, change something, such as a shirt button, your position (from lying down to sitting up), or where you are in the room. Call your child back into the room. When he returns, see if he can see what's different.

Play as subtly (untie one shoe) or as broadly (move to another chair across the room) as the child can handle.

Have You Seen My Friend?

DIRECTIONS

Player A goes up to player B and says "Have you seen my friend?" Player B asks, "What does your friend look like?" Player A describes someone in the group, giving details such as height, weight, hair color, type of clothes. Player B guesses who the friend is. Player B gets five guesses, or any other number you think appropriate.

VARIATIONS

♦ Player A gives subtle clues at first, such as "She has hair," followed by more ("She has brown hair") and more specific clues ("She has on a striped shirt").

♦ If Player B guesses correctly, he has to chase the identified friend to a specific spot. If he catches her before reaching that spot, the friend becomes the next Player A.

Run Wild, Run Free

This game requires vision in the midst of distractions. It also releases excess energy when the children need to "let go."

I found that Run Wild, Run Free is one of those games that the kids never tire of. To put it another way, it is a game that I tire of before they do.

Be inconsistent about how much time is spent running wild and free so the children really have to keep half an eye on the chief. Compliment the behavior you want. "You sat down so fast! Good watching!"

A lot of children want to be the chief (surprise, surprise). In this variation, many get to be chief for at least one round.

DIRECTIONS

Explain that you are the chief, and the children are members of your family. You have a fine life together running free in the jungle except that there is one danger—tigers. The way the children keep from being eaten by a tiger is to watch the wise chief. Like all chiefs, you have magic ears and hear the tiger before anyone else. When the chief sits down with hand over mouth, everyone else immediately sits down, too. This quietness fools the tiger, who goes away. The chief signals the all clear by yelling, "Run wild, run free!" Everyone (especially the chief) starts whooping, hollering, jumping, running, and having a good time. Then, plop, the chief suddenly sits down again. Instantly everyone else does, too. Repeat until everyone seems sufficiently tired.

VARIATION

♦ If you are playing with a large group, do not let anyone except the chief know who is chief. An easy way of picking the chief without anyone knowing is to have the children stand with their backs to you. You walk behind them and quietly touch the back of the chief for that game.

Everyone has to watch everyone else to see who sits down first. This is a good exercise in peripheral awareness.

What's Here?

This would just be a fun activity with a little one. One- to four-year-olds couldn't care less that there is no point to it. Just say, "Let's feel!" and go from thing to thing, feeling it.

DIRECTIONS

Children feel different things in the room with their fingertips and talk about how the objects feel and how they differ from each other.

Example

Compare the smooth desktop to the wall texture, the leather coat to the cotton one, the pen to the pencil.

"Let's go feel the refrigerator." Then, go feel it, rub it, pat it, bang out a rhythm on it together. Then, "Let's go feel the velvet pillow," and go rub it against your faces, your arms, your thighs. Make the sound that comes to you when you feel something so soft. Rub, pat, squeeze, toss. "This is how soft things feel."

Remember to ask, "What shall we go feel next?" so your child gets practice making choices.

Hot Coals

Invite your child to sit quietly and imagine what the following things would feel like. Read the list aloud slowly.

◇ A hot coal

◇ A snuggly bear rug

◇ A prickly bush

◇ A soft pillow

◇ A piece of ice

◇ Bare feet on spring grass

◇ Bare feet in mud

Bag Heads

DIRECTIONS

Put a bag over one child's head. Everyone else runs around until the Bag Head says, "Freeze." Everyone stays where they are while the Bag Head wanders around trying to find someone. When he does, he has to guess who it is by touch. If the guess is correct, that person becomes a Bag Head, too, and they both go looking for new people to identify. If the guess is incorrect, everyone gets to run around again until the Bag Head calls out "Freeze" again and tries again. The game continues until all but one person have bags over their heads. The last person identified becomes the first Bag Head for the next game.

Materials

Several paper grocery bags

If the Bag Heads are having a hard time finding people because the room is so large, reduce the size of the boundaries. Many times I find that instead of trying *not* to be tagged, players seek it. Some people just like to have a bag over their head. Go figure.

Guess Who

I have played this game with three- and four-year-olds at a Headstart program and found that they were good at identifying and jumped around in excitement waiting for their turns to be guessers.

CHANT

Who is this, who is this?

Can you tell me who is this?

DIRECTIONS

One player is blindfolded or has a bag over her head. Everyone chants the chant as you guide one person in front of the blindfolded player, who feels the person and guesses who it is.

VARIATION

♦ This is an especially good variation to do with older people. I have played it in a nursing facility where people are not touched nearly enough. Whenever the group got together for game time, this was one of the games they wanted to play.

Instead of feeling the whole person, just feel hands instead. Start the game by allowing everyone to feel each other's hands. Some hands are long and slender, others firm and thick, have different temperatures and differing degrees of dryness.

What Is This?

CHANT

What is this, what is this?

Can you tell me what is this?

DIRECTIONS

Tell your child that you are each going to collect a bunch of little things such as paper clips, spoons, buttons, pens, spools. Keep your objects a secret from each other by holding them behind your back, or putting them in a bag, or in your pockets. Then take turns being blindfolded and presenting one of your objects to the blindfolded person. Try to guess what they are.

Draw a Letter

DIRECTIONS

Draw a letter or number on each other's backs and try to guess which specific one was drawn.

Logs to Market

Enjoy the sensation of being in close contact. Do not worry about kids squashing each other. Even a little person can take the weight of a big person for a short time. All belt buckles and spiked jewelry have to be removed, of course.

DIRECTIONS

Children pretend they are logs and lie beside each other. With a little help from you, the first "log" rolls over the second log and then rolls over all the others until the end of the line. Then the second log does the same thing and the game continues until all the logs have had a turn.

VARIATION

♦ The first child lies across and on top of the other children's bodies and all the children on the bottom roll continually. Their rolling gives the first person a ride from one end of the group to the other! (You have to try this. It's unusual fun!)

Taster

Smell gives us clues to how things taste. You cannot tell a raw potato from an apple without the use of smell.

DIRECTIONS

Have several items ready for a taste test. Ask your child to close her eyes and hold her nose. One by one, give her small tastes to see if she can identify the items.

Ask which part of the tongue is most responsive. Sweet on the tip? Salty on the sides?

Materials

Safe items to be tasted

Flavorings

Materials

Those nice little brown bottles that hold different flavorings such as vanilla, peppermint, licorice, and lemon

DIRECTIONS

Hold a bottle so the label can't be seen, and open it. (Try not to see the label beforehand yourself.) Smell it yourself first and then put it under your child's nose. Ask what smell she thinks it is. Then try another and another.

Sniff It

Materials

Coffee, dish soap, bar soap, perfume, soy sauce, mustard, other common household items

DIRECTIONS

See how many smells your child can identify with his eyes closed.

Memory Smells

Items that are likely to carry memories, such as a cologne or perfume you once wore, a particular kind of soap, clothes, a plastic inner tube, a favorite kind of candy, or cinnamon, popcorn, lavender—any smell that has been in the family's life.

DIRECTIONS

With your child, choose an item, shut your eyes, smell deeply, and then talk about the memory associated with that smell. Invite your child to do the same.

See, Hear, Say

DIRECTIONS

Face each other. On the count of three, you both put your hands over your ears, your eyes, or your mouth. The object is to see how often you both choose the same position at the same time.

VARIATION

Do you know the hand game Scissors, Paper, Rock? Instead of trying to win, try to come up with the same symbol and match each other! (See page 142 for Scissors, Paper, Rock instructions.)

Make Believe Memories

This is a good game to play with people who may not know each other well.

DIRECTIONS

Each person puts something in the bag that has some personal meaning—for example, a ring, a favorite pen, a lucky coin.

Each player takes one of the items that is not their own, holds it in his or her hand, and after a while, makes up a story about the item, such as when it was first used or where it came from.

The story, of course, will probably not be true, but will be delightful to the owner, true or not.

Example

"This is a ring that was given to a man by his grandmother because she wanted him to always be in touch with his land of birth."

VARIATION

♦ After the made-up story, the owner tells a true story about the item.

Day Dream Time

Take time each day just to stare off into space.

Use the time for joyful anticipation—imagining seeing a friend again or a summer vacation at a lake. Try channeling your daydreams into visualizations, such as imagining playing a sport in order to improve your game.

Children daydream naturally. This game honors that and makes time for it.

DIRECTIONS

With your child, lie down on a rug, turn the lights down low, and have soft music playing. Encourage your child to let her mind wander wherever it takes her. Explain that this is a private time. No talking is permitted so you both can follow your own thoughts.

VARIATIONS

◆ Encourage a particular kind of daydreaming, such as visualization. For instance, imagine doing his best in the school play tomorrow or doing a trick he's been trying to do on the jungle gym.

◆ Sit in front of the windows, if you have pleasant views. Suggest that rather than look at anything in detail, it would be fun to let your eyes rest, unfocused. Just relax and feel the whole scene. If your child would rather follow the antics of a squirrel in a tree, that's okay, too.

Chapter 6

MY BODY

I spend a lot of time with young children working to improve their coordination. I call it "recess prep." They practice catching and throwing, walking balance beams, and changing directions while running fast. I want children to know their bodies—and be good at recess games and other physical activities!

There is great joy in movement. If you are happy in your body—whether you love to do heavy physical labor or to climb—jump hurrah!

Can You Do What I Do?

CHANT

Can you do what _____ does?

Can you do what _____ does?

1 2 3 4 5 6 7 8

DIRECTIONS

Chant (or sing making up your own tune or using a familiar jingle) between each person's turn. Each time, insert a player's name. While the group counts aloud, that person does a movement, such as snapping fingers, alternating hands, stomping feet.

Start by taking your turn first (in fact, take several turns and demonstrate a variety of possible movements).

If you are playing with a group, continue with either the child next to you or, if you would rather, choose among the children who want to be next. Remember, there is no way to fail. If someone stands (or sits) with one hand between the legs and the other on the mouth, that's an original, personal movement, too. I have never seen a child insulted by imitation. It is empowering to have everyone do what you do.

Example

Can you do what Mei does?

Can you do what Mei does?

1 2 3 4 5 6 7 8

Mei might twirl around. Then the group would sing, "Can you do what Hans does," and Hans might jump up and down. Then the group would sing, "Can you do what Manny does. . . ." During Manny's eight counts he, not being in a terribly original mood, would jump up and down, too. When John, on his turn, starts jumping up and down, it's a good time to say something like "Let's jump and turn," or "jump and clap," or "jump and pat our tummy," or "What else can we do beside jumping? What about kicking, turning, swinging, nodding, hopping, swaying, or clapping?"

After playing a few rounds, the kids can become very original in their movements.

Up and Down

This game enhances body awareness by isolating muscle groups. If you have burned out on Hokey Pokey and shaking it all about, this might be the game for you.

CHANT

Up and down and up and down,

See our feet go up and down.

DIRECTIONS

Get in a sitting position with legs stretched out in front.

Chant together while your feet are alternately flexing and pointing. Next add:

Up and down and up and down,

See our legs go up and down.

Legs then do their thing and go up and down on cue. I go from a straight leg to a bent one.

Then go on to the trunk (call it "body" rather than trunk, though, or you will end up hearing elephant jokes), then do the arms, hands, shoulders and head, flexing and extending each appropriately. End with the eyes going up and down; eye muscles need a workout, too.

VARIATIONS

♦ Do the whole series over again with these words:

Side to side and side to side,

See our feet (legs, knees, trunk, arms, hands, shoulders, head)

Go side to side.

♦ If the group is ready to add another skill, the whole series can be done with this variation:

Round and round and round and round,

See our feet (etc.) go round and round.

Add all body parts that can rotate. Straight legs rotate from the hip joints, arms from the shoulder, trunk from the waist and ankles and wrists from their joints.

♦ For an added challenge, I like to add eyes to the end of each series as in "eyes also go side to side" or "round and round."

Hello, Good-bye

Since rhythm is so closely linked with reading, speaking, and smooth movements, it's helpful to slip in rhythm whenever you can.

CHANT

Hello, good-bye.

Hello, good-bye, hello.

DIRECTIONS

Feet and hands flex on "hello," and extend on "good-bye."

Sit with legs straight in front and flex the feet saying "hello." Then point the feet and say "good-bye." Repeat many times, encouraging your child to imitate you. Once he starts to get it, alternate with a rhythmic pattern.

Example

"Hello" (pause while feet flex), "good-bye" (pause while feet point).

"Hello, good-bye, hello" (feet flex, point, flex in quick succession).

Repeat and repeat until it has gotten so easy that boredom is just about to set in, then switch to—the hands!

Extended hands say hello, flexed hands say good-bye.

VARIATIONS

♦ Say "hello" and "good-bye" with the hands and feet at the same time.

♦ Say "hello" with the feet while saying "good-bye" with the hands and then reverse.

♦ Have the right side of the body (foot and hand) do hellos and the left side do good-byes and then switch back and forth. This will take some mental focusing that is always good practice.

♦ Have the right hand and the left foot say "hello," while the left hand and the right foot say "good-bye." This encourages coordination of both sides of the body.

♦ Sit with legs straight out as before but with your body flexed forward with the head touching the knees (or as close as you can come to your knees). Sit up sharply on the "hello" and bend the torso back on the "good-bye." Come up quickly to a straight back on the next "hello" and go back to the original head to knee position on the next "goodbye." This is a good total wake-up-the-body-first-thing-in-the-morning exercise. It also works on balance and abdominal strength. Remind your child to make his "tummy tight" from leaning forward to straight up and from leaning back to straight up. The tummy muscles help pull her up.

Starting position

Hello!

Goodbye!

Hello!

Neat Feet

This game is good for the very young and is done seated in chairs with feet flat on the floor or seated on the floor with knees bent and feet flat on the floor.

CHANT

> Feet feet feet feet—
>
> Isn't it neat to have some feet?
>
> Right foot, (stomp),
>
> Left foot, (stomp),
>
> Loud feet (stomp loudly), soft feet (stomp softly).

DIRECTIONS

Stomp your feet on the floor while chanting.

Keep repeating until all or most of the group is copying you, then switch to:

> Right foot (stomp, stomp, stomp, stomp, stomp, stomp, stomp, stomp).
>
> Left foot (stomp for eight beats total, too).
>
> Fast feet (stomp quickly).
>
> S-l-o-w feet (stomp in slow motion).

VARIATION

◆ Hand hand hands hands—

Isn't it grand to have some hands?

One hand (slapping it on the floor or lap for eight beats).

The other hand (do the same).

Both hands (eight beats).

What Can Your Head Do?

Did you notice that each joint has specific movements? Knee joints, unlike arm joints, for instance, cannot go round and round, just up and down.

DIRECTIONS

Begin talking about all the things the body can do, starting with the head. Go down the body—head, shoulders, arms, chest, hips, legs, knees, ankles, and toes—demonstrating how each moves. Say:

◇ "What can the head do? It can go from side to side, up and down, and all around." Do each movement together.

◇ "What can the shoulders do? They can shrug (go up and down) and go back and forward together and individually." Do each movement together.

Arms

This is a quick little game to insert in between other games. Everybody always wants to try it.

DIRECTIONS

Start with arms straight over head, hands and fingers extended. Drop fingers from the knuckles and then the hands from the wrist while the arms are still straight. Then drop the forearms, then the whole arms.

Build back up. First the elbows come up, then the forearms, then the wrist. Then stretch out the fingers until the arms are in their original position again.

Toes, Knees, Hips, and Clap

If you have been hanging around kindergartners, you know this favorite song:

> *Head, Shoulder, Knees and Toes—Knees and Toes.*
> *Head, Shoulder, Knees and Toes—Knees and Toes.*
> *Knees and Tooooes.*
> *Eyes and Ears and Mouth and Nose.*
> *Head, Shoulder, Knees and Toes—Knees and Toes.*

If your child is not quite ready for the Head, Shoulder, Knees and Toes song, chant this abbreviated version.

CHANT

> Toes, knees, hips, and clap!
> Toes, knees, hips, and clap!
> Toes, knees, hips, and clap!
> Eyes and ears and nose.
> Toes, knees, hips, and clap!

DIRECTIONS

Touch the body parts as you mention them.

Boop Boop Be Doop

This simple chant is for the young ones who are just learning about names of body parts. The words are inspired by Betty Boop, a cartoon figure from the '30s.

CHANT

Put your hands on your head, boop boop be doop.

Put your hands on your eyes, boop boop be doop.

Put your hands on your ears, boop boop be doop.

Put your hands on your neck, boop boop be doop.

Put your hands on your shoulders, boop boop be doop.

Put your hands on your legs, boop boop be doop. (etc., etc.)

DIRECTIONS

Do what you say! As your child learns, add words like eyebrows, knuckles, or esophagus.

Let's Walk in a Circle

If you are playing with a group of children, this is a good way to get everyone going.

CHANT

Let's walk in a circle,

Let's walk in a circle,

Let's walk in a circle,

And let's do it right now!

Let's walk way down low,

Way down low,

Way down low, and we're

Doing it right now!

Let's walk way up high,

Way up high,

Way up high,

And let's do it right now!

DIRECTIONS

Begin chanting the first verse.

When everyone is comfortably walking around in a circle, add the second verse.

This verse is accompanied by walking in a squat position. It adds humor if you also lower and deepen your voice. Do this as many times as your group can tolerate having thighs strengthen.

Then switch to the third verse. Do not forget to use a squeaky high voice, if you are playfully inclined.

VARIATIONS

◆ Walk on your heels, Walk on your toes, Walk on the insides of your feet, Walk on the outsides of your feet.

◆ Walk real loud (stamp your feet loudly), Walk real soft (tiptoe).

◆ FREEZE. I use the command, "Freeze," as a transition between movements, especially between walking forward and walking backward. That way, kids won't bang into each other if part of the group gets what they are suppose to do immediately and the others miss it by a beat or two. It's also a good transitional move between walking fast and walking slowly or to get back control after walking "real silly." Letting chaos reign for a few moments can reduce tension from the day.

◆ Walk backwards, Walk sideways, Walk real fast, Walk real slow (in slow motion).

◆ Walk real silly (anything goes here).

◆ Walk like a robot (arm and leg on one side alternate with other arm and leg).

◆ Walk like a soldier (opposite arm with leg or cross lateral walk). Switching from robot to soldier is a good lesson in integrating both sides of the body.

◆ Walk like a rag doll (limp and floppy); walk like the Tin Man (straight and stiff). Doing opposite movements can help children be aware of the difference between muscle tension and relaxation.

♦ If any children are in wheelchairs, include movements like

"Let's roll in a circle."

"Head goes up and down."

"Blink your eyes."

"Stick your tongue out."

Eight Beats

This game, which is easy to catch on to, encourages large motor movements and rhythm. You can also encourage originality if you ask others to come up with variations.

CHANT

Clap, 2, 3, 4, 5, 6, 7, 8 (clapping on each number)

Jump, 2, 3, 4, 5, 6, 7, 8 (jumping on each number)

Hop, 2, 3, 4, 5, 6, 7, 8

Bounce, 2, 3, 4, 5, 6, 7, 8

Twirl, 2, 3, 4, 5, 6, 7, 8

DIRECTIONS

Give and follow your chant, doing what you say. If you have encouraged your child to add her ideas, you might hear "shrug," "shake," "wiggle," "vibrate," or any other variation. Also, try "scan" or "stare." Stare is always good for a giggle as people experience getting in the spotlight of a stare.

VARIATION

♦ To include a physically challenged child, try "blink," "nod," or "move leg."

Pick an Apple

This game is good for stretching the body and the imagination. Of course, the tree does not have to be an apple tree. In the tropics, I play Pick a Mango.

CHANT

(Make up your own tune if you prefer to sing.)

Pick an apple,

Pick an apple.

Put it in the box.

Pick an apple,

Pick an apple,

Put it in the box.

DIRECTIONS

Tell your child to imagine a large apple tree right before his eyes. All he has to do is reach up way, way high to pick apples, and then bend down from the waist to put them in a box. Then chant the words while he does the movements. Encourage him to really stretch and reach for the highest apple, and then say:

"We got every apple from that tree. Let's go look for another (miming these actions). Let's walk down the road, jump over the creek, climb up the hill, crawl under the fence, and here's the next tree!" Start all over again, chanting and reaching.

Stand Up, Sit Down

This is a mildly dumb game, but it's good for warming up the total body, and children seem to find it amusing. Warning: It might not have the same effect on adults; one adult said her thighs hurt for a couple of days after. (I should have warned her ahead of time). The kids, however, had no complaints.

DIRECTIONS

If everyone is seated, ask them to stand. When they are standing, say something like, "Oh, I changed my mind, let's sit down." Once they are seated, act like the absentminded professor, saying, "Oh, wait a minute. I forgot. Let's stand up after all." When they are standing, say, "Why don't we just sit down?" Then speed up the action to an interplay of standing and sitting until everyone is laughing and feeling nicely goofy. By then you will have won their attention and affection because they want to see what you'll come up with next.

I Can't, I Can

DIRECTIONS

Be seated slumped over, side by side. Heads, shoulders, arms are all dragging. Say the words, "I can't do it. It's too hard, I am too small. I can't. I just can't." Then switch your posture to a straight trunk, shoulders back, chin up, and say, "Yes, I can! I can do it! I can learn, I do know. I am smart,

I can do it!" Then switch back again to the slumped position with the same sort of defeated words: "No, I can't; it's too hard."

Go back and forth with this for a while, ending, of course, with the positive position.

Seed to Flower to Seed

Tell your child that you are both going to be seeds that s-l-o-w-l-y unfold to become flowers, and see what happens.

DIRECTIONS

Take a slumped over position, all curled up, legs crossed; or kneel. Let an arm pop up to be an emerging leaf, and the back straighten to be a stem. Then let the other arm become another new leaf. Finally, hold both arms straight and stretched high with your head back. Pretend to be a blossom with its face in the glorious sunshine. Then the flower drops its seeds, slowly wilts, and dies by doing the original movements in reverse—returning to the earth only to be reborn from seed in the spring. In this game, spring comes around about a minute later!

VARIATIONS

♦ When your blossoms bloom, let a friend or siblings go around with a pretend sprinkling can and water your faces.

♦ Going from a cocoon to a caterpillar to a butterfly encourages a whole different range of movements. Let your child improvise.

We Are Rocking

This game works on balance and motor control, the ability to maintain your center, and the ability to stop your body once it is in motion.

CHANT

I am rocking, rocking, rocking.

I am rocking.

Now I'm still.

(FREEZE)

DIRECTIONS

Stand with legs together or slightly apart and begin to rock sideways while chanting.

On the word "still," "freeze" in an upright or tilted position, finding your center of balance in whatever position you happen to be. Repeat the chant.

Rock a little farther and a little harder each time. Keep increasing the difficulty until it looks as things might get out of hand. Once you have rocked as far as possible and before silliness sets in, ask your child to switch positions.

VARIATIONS

♦ Besides rocking side to side, rock front to back. Other possible positions are: kneeling, sitting with legs outstretched or cross-legged or any of the previous positions with eyes closed. The rocking can be forward and backward or side to side in these different positions.

♦ Change the chant to cover different movements, such as "I am jumping," "I am hopping," "I am skipping." These movements work on motor control and balance, too.

♦ When children are in the "freeze" or "still" position, it's an added challenge to go around and gently try to push them off balance so they can practice keeping control of their center.

♦ Chant silently. You may find that one person is moving and another "freezing" at the same time.

Did You Ever See a Lassie?

To play this game, it helps to be familiar with the song. By the way, "lassie" refers to a Scottish girl and not to a dog.

CHANT

Did you ever see a lassie

Go this way and that way?

Did you ever see a lassie

Go this way and that?

This way and that way

And this way and that way—

Did you ever see a lassie

Go this way and that?

DIRECTIONS

Start by choosing and doing a movement that goes with the easy rhythm of the song. Ask your group to imitate you. Then ask for the others to take turns by saying, for example, "Have you ever seen a Christy go this way (and so on)." Keep substituting the name of each child in the verse. The other children do whatever movements Christy (or whoever) does.

Simon Does

This is similar to Simon Says, except there is no trick to it. It can be done in a group with everyone having a turn to be Simon. It can be done with just two people mirroring each other. It can even be done with just one and a mirror because it is good feedback to see how a movement feels and looks.

D IRECTIONS

Everybody moves the way Simon moves as if they were mirror reflections of him. Simon might try awkward and strange—maybe even contorted—poses sometimes just to get the others to really notice how his body moves.

Add a Move

D IRECTIONS

If you have a group, have the first person do a movement, any movement, then have each person add a movement. Then put all the movements together and do them as a dance having, if possible, each movement flow into the next.

To make the flowing part happen more easily, have each person take the finished stance of the person before and start there.

PART THREE

Sharing Who I Am!

Chapter 7

TELLING OTHERS

We are all living novels. The stories of our lives are continually being written: who we are, where we came from, what we are doing, where we are going, our hopes, our dreams, our realities. . . .

Games like these give children ways to tell their stories.

When You Get Up in the Morning

SONG

(To the tune of "When the Bear Went Over the Mountain")
When you get up in the morning,
When you get up in the morning,
When you get up in the morning,
Show us what you do.

DIRECTIONS

Sing the song together, then mime your morning activities such as stretching, rolling out of bed, or brushing your teeth. Sing the song again, then let your child take a turn miming something different, such as showering or getting dressed. Repeat as many times as you enjoy.

VARIATIONS

Using the same tune and format, sing:

♦ "When you get home from school (repeat three times), show us what you do."

♦ "When you come to school . . . show us what you do."

♦ "Before you go to bed . . . show us what you do."

♦ "When you go on a vacation . . . show us what you do," and so on.

What Are the Things You Like to Do?

CHANT

(To the tune "Mary Had a Little Lamb")

What are things you like to do,

Like to do,

Like to do,

What are things you like to do,

Won't you show us now?

DIRECTIONS

After each repetition of the song, take turns miming answers and guessing what's going on.

VARIATIONS

♦ What are ways you like to move?

♦ Where are places you like to go?

♦ What will you be when you're grown up?

♦ What are things you love to eat?

Happies Are Big

CHANT

Happies are big.

Happies are small.

What makes you happiest of all?

DIRECTIONS

Here's a chance for children to tell each other the big or little things that make them happiest, like going to grandma's or petting the cat.

Morning, Morning

SONG

(To the tune "Twinkle, Twinkle Little Star")

Morning, morning,

Break of day—

Tell us how you

Start your day.

DIRECTIONS

After each repetition of the song, one of the players talks about her morning.

VARIATIONS

◆ This evening version is for the older child. Younger children may need some help with sequencing the events of the day, even though they love to hear their whole day recalled.

Evening, evening,

End of day—

Tell us how you

Spent your day.

♦ If you want children to mime how they spend their morning or how they spent their day, change the line from "Tell us how . . ." to "Show us how. . . ."

Favorite Fruit

CHANT

Fruit, fruit is good to eat.

Which fruit is your favorite treat?

DIRECTIONS

Pretend there is a pile of fruit in front of you. One by one, after the chant, pretend to choose a piece of fruit from the center and take a bite, peeling or cutting or doing whatever is necessary to reach the fruit. Children try to guess which fruit is being eaten.

VARIATION

♦ Here's a fun way to introduce people in a group. After choosing and guessing the fruit, the fruit eater gets to introduce himself using his fruit as his last name. If I chose a banana I would say, "I am Barbara Banana." If I chose a watermelon, I would say, "I am Barbara Watermelon."

See how easy it is to remember Joe Grape and Mary Mango.

I've Got a Rhythm Inside of Me

We tend to like rhythms that match our mood and general style. For example, expect a slow, steady beat from the child who happens to be a slow, steady type and a hyped-up, more staccato beat from the quicker-moving child.

CHANT

I've got a rhythm inside of me

That goes like this . . .

DIRECTIONS

Repeat the chant together with your child. Take your turn pounding out a rhythm on the floor with your hands or feet while your child imitates it. Chant again before your child takes her turn.

Dreams

Dreams are a way of knowing our unconscious selves. This game encourages children to value and to remember their dream time.

CHANT

Dreams are scary.

Dreams are fun.

You had a dream,

So tell us one.

DIRECTIONS

Chant together, then take turns sharing the dreams that you remember.

Wishes

Every dream that comes true starts with a wish!

CHANT

"When you wish upon a star"

DIRECTIONS

Sing or chant the first line to Jiminy Cricket's song from *Pinocchio* between turns. After each chant, take turns talking about your wishes, whatever they are. Do you want to colonize Mars? Does your child want to go to Disneyland, eat a lug of cherries, be the fastest runner in the world?

Future Occupations

A young girl once asked me if she could be a clown, a writer, and a teacher. "Absolutely," I replied.

CHANT

Dooby dooby dooby de,
Show us who you'd like to be.

DIRECTIONS

Chant between each person's turn. Act out your answers (or just say the words). If players complain that they do not know what they want to be, they can show an occupation they admire.

Present Skills

It's truly amazing how much children learn to do in a few short years. By the time many children are four years old, they think they know more than anyone else! This chant gives children a chance to show off some of their knowledge.

CHANT

Cooby cooby cooby coo,

Show us what you've learned to do.

DIRECTIONS

After each chant, take turns walking, hopping, riding a bike, writing cursive, doing somersaults, doing 'itsy bitsy spider," or whatever else.

Drawing Together

When I was a young girl, my sister and I went to visit an aunt who lived in a town a few hours away from our home. She was in her twenties and pregnant with her first child.

On our first day together, my sister and I lay on the floor coloring when something totally unexpected happened. My aunt got down on the floor with us and starting coloring, too! I was thrilled and shocked. I did not know adults did such things.

Adults who do, know this wonderful thing about drawing with a child: Even if your stick figures look pathetic, children do not judge. They are amazed if a drawing actually looks like anything they recognize, and supportive if it does not, because they are simply glad that you are doing this work together. A thousand sets of clean dishes will not replace that kind of warmth.

DIRECTIONS

Leave the dishes in the sink and draw together.

VARIATIONS

♦ Make a homemade book together about things your child likes. The illustrations can be pictures cut out of magazines, photographs, or drawings of your favorite things and his. You can call the book, "Things *We* Like."

♦ Work on the same picture together, each adding different details. For example, make the circle for the face. She adds the eyes. You add the nose. She adds the body. You do legs and so on until you have put in the details of buttons and bows or whole background scenes.

My Life

Older children like making albums complete with text and drawings. They usually enjoy sharing their albums with their friends.

DIRECTIONS

Here are some possible "chapter" titles:

◊ Where I live: Describe or draw pictures of your house and surroundings. Describe the outside, make a floor plan of the inside, or both.

◊ Where I live (the big picture): This can include the village, city, state, country, and galaxy!

◊ Who I live with: Pictures, drawing, descriptions, stories about and attitudes toward the family could be included here.

◊ Where I've been: Include travels as well as local excursions.

◊ Where I go to school (if outside the home)

◊ Places I go in town

◊ Neighbors and relatives

◊ Favorite restaurants

◊ Best playground

◊ Summer spots (pool, lake, swimming hole)

Materials

Pencils, paper, crayons, markers, photos

My Story

This is a tale that starts from the moment of birth.

DIRECTIONS

Help your child narrate his own history. The narrative can be written, dictated, or recorded on tape, touching on these subjects and any others that occur to you:

Materials

Pencils and paper, or computer or tape recorder

◇ Where were you born?

◇ Who else is in your family?

◇ Describe your mom, dad, siblings, or whoever is in your family.

◇ What is your first memory?

◇ What other childhood memories do you have? Anything scary? Anything especially wonderful?

◇ What were some important events in your life? What did they mean to you?

◇ What are your wishes?

My Family

One does not have to be related by blood—or even be a human—to be considered part of the family. This activity encourages children to interview their elders and gain a broader view of their ancestors' hopes, dreams and traditions.

DIRECTIONS

Materials

Pencil and paper, or computer or tape recorder

Help your child make a book about the family. Topics could include:

◇ A word or two about each family member

◇ Things we do when we are together

◇ What matters to us

◇ Where our ancestors lived

◇ Traditions and stories that were passed down

◇ Foods we often eat

◇ Foods we serve for special occasions

◇ What our grandparents' (or other elder relatives) lives were like

A Letter to Me

What if around birthday time, you always wrote a letter to your future self and kept the letter to read on your next birthday? You would probably see your growth and gain a sense of continuity.

I remember my surprise at reading an old diary of mine. I suddenly realized that I had learned a lesson back then that I was in the process of relearning. "You mean I already know that?" I exclaimed to myself. It helped me see that we keep learning in different ways until we finally get it!

Materials

Pencil and paper, or computer or tape recorder

DIRECTIONS

Help your child or children write or dictate a letter to themselves. They might want to cover topics such as:

◇ Their interests

◇ Their friends

◇ What they most like to do

◇ Where they like to go

◇ What books, television shows, food, game are their favorites now

◇ What they hope will happen to them

My Week or Month

DIRECTIONS

Each person collects different things during the week or month that are reminders of what happened, such as a rock from a walk, a pamphlet from the dentist's office, a candy wrapper, a movie ticket, and so on.

At the end of the period, schedule a time when you gather together to "show and tell" with any or all of your stuff.

How Do You Express Yourself?

Each person has a unique way of expressing things.

DIRECTIONS

Using your bodies as well as your voices, take turns expressing the following:

◇ Words: yes, no, why, stop, me, you, together, wow, help, or other words you like

◇ Phrases: go away, you make me sick, I want you, don't leave me, I am hungry, you are beautiful, I am in love, I don't understand, you are so nice, I hate you, I love you

◇ Characters: old dignified woman, bag lady, young girl, young boy, baby, toddler just learning to walk, Santa Claus, coal miner, logger, fat man

People Sorting

This game encourages children to think about the kinds of things they prefer and gives them a chance to experiment with not going along with the gang.

DIRECTIONS

The leader makes up categories and the players respond accordingly. Children must choose among the possibilities offered, unless you want to offer an "all of the above" or "none of the above" option. Start off with simple obvious distinctions, such as physical attributes (dark hair, light hair, medium hair, blue eyes, brown eyes, other colors) to get the idea of the game going. It's helpful to have your categories made up ahead of time so that you can say them quickly. You want the children to respond instantly from their gut and not from their head by watching what others do first.

Examples

◇ "Everyone who likes breakfast best stands over here and people who like lunch best stand over there and people who like them both the same stand in the middle."

◇ "Everyone who likes to read stories stands there, those who would rather write stories stand there, and those who like them both the same stand here."

◇ "If you enjoy playing by yourself, stand by the window. If you'd rather play with one or two others, stand by the couch, and if you like playing with groups, stand by the table."

◇ Other possibilities:

- ♦ Prefer to hike in the forest, swim in the ocean, or climb a mountain
- ♦ Prefer to swim in the ocean, swim in a lake, or swim in a pool
- ♦ Prefer to eat fruit, vegetables, or grains
- ♦ Prefer bubble gum, sugarless gum, or regular gum
- ♦ Prefer sleeping, running, or dancing
- ♦ Prefer working on a computer, in a garden, or on a hobby

VARIATIONS

♦ Make up other choices with the children. Don't be afraid to stretch. Some possibilities:

◇ Futuristic, such as to start a colony on Mars, travel to Pluto, or program spaceships from Earth

◇ Fanciful, such as to be an ant, a hippopotamus, or a koala bear

◇ Preposterous, such as to be a pencil, a typewriter, or a computer

Sculptor

In this game, one person moves another in much the same way a window dresser would move a mannequin.

DIRECTIONS

Take turns with your child being the sculptor and being the sculpture.

Moving arms, legs, head, fingers, the "sculptor" can name his sculpture or just talk about how it felt to be the one who does the moving. The "sculpture" can talk about how it felt to be moved.

Things I Know

Surveys show that standing in front of an audience and talking is almost as stressful as moving or getting a divorce.

If children practice talking about topics they enjoy, they will be more comfortable making speeches in school or when they are grown-ups.

DIRECTIONS

What will a child want to discuss? Introduce the following topics to stimulate your young speech maker:

◇ Things I know that my parents don't
◇ The coolest place I've ever been
◇ Why I like (or don't like) the way gymnasiums smell
◇ What my little (brother, sister) needs to know
◇ Why I am smarter than my older (brother, sister)
◇ My favorite kind of nose booger
◇ Things I do best
◇ The worst thing in the world
◇ If I were in charge, I would—

Chapter 8

BEING WITH FRIENDS

We may not control how our children make friends, but we can help. We can invite playmates to the house when they are young and make arrangements to be part of parent-child playgroups or homeschool. We can host birthday parties and holiday events. We can volunteer in the school and even lead or work with the local Scouts or 4-H. We can help our children learn to interact with others by playing group games like these.

Balloon

DIRECTIONS

Ask the group to hold hands and form a close circle around one person who stands in the middle. Tell them that she is going to be the "blower" and they are going to be her balloon. She then pretends to blow up a balloon. As she blows, the others make the circle bigger and bigger, until they no longer can hold hands. At that point, the balloon bursts and all the kids, pretending they are pieces of a busted balloon, twirl around and fall down. You can give the clues when to fall down.

You will find that everyone wants a turn to be the blower. If you have a large group, let a few kids play blower at the same time.

VARIATION

♦ With older kids, pretend the circle is a lake. The person in the center is the rain pouring, causing a flood, or the wind blowing hot air and causing a drought. The lake grows and shrinks accordingly. Remember to take a swim in the full lake by doing the backstroke and sidestroke, too! If the group is having a hard time staying together, it's helpful to say, "We need each one of you to make a perfect circle. No one can do it alone. Let's all grow and shrink together."

Ring Around the Rosy

No, I am not going to tell you how to play this ancient game. I am just going to suggest that instead of ending with "we all fall down," you try variations.

CHANT

Ring around the rosy,
A pocket full of posies,
Ashes, ashes,
All jump up!

DIRECTIONS

Take suggestions from the group so everyone gets a turn to add a new ending to an old favorite. The ending can also be designed to fit the skills of a physically challenged player. Some possible endings are:

Examples

"We all jump around"

"We all say hello"

"We all bend over"

"We all hop on one foot"

Aunt Sophie Died

Children seem to like this one quite a lot, although it seems mildly morbid. You might check to see if any of the children actually has an Aunt Sophie and if so, change the name to Aunt Myrtle or Aunt Dinah or something like Aunt Mushibadaby.

If the children are very young and have just learned about death, they might not think this game is funny. However, if they are eight and older and have seen that death is a part of life, then they will relish it. It's a kind of "laugh in the face of death," a survivor's bravado.

DIRECTIONS

Someone says, "My Aunt Sophie died."

The group responds:

"Ohhhhh—how'd she die?"

And the player says,

"She died doing this."

The person makes whatever movement he wants to, however stupid or however coordinated, although "silly" is more typical. Everyone imitates what is done before the next person has a turn.

VARIATION

♦ You can achieve the same amount of silliness (which is a form of letting go and releasing tension and a chance to follow no rules) by doing the rondo that goes:

> Dilly Dilly Pick a Lily,
>
> Can you show us something silly?

They will.

Walk This Way

To play this game when my daughters were young, we would walk like a giant, taking great big steps, and then walk like a fairy, taking lots of itsy-bitsy steps. As the girls grew a little older, we switched to trying simple dance steps for each other to imitate. We grew very comfortable with this game. One day when they were young teenagers, we were walking down a country road with their new friends. I started to play the game to make the walk feel shorter. Their new friends, surprisingly, got right into it. I was delighted that they wanted to be playful, too, and glad that I could interact with my cool teenagers.

DIRECTIONS

One person takes a turn as a leader and walks in whatever style he or she wants. It could be a standard movement like skipping or jumping, or it could be a made-up step like a shuffle to the left and then a shuffle to the right. Everyone has to imitate these movements, and everyone gets a turn to be the leader.

Tricky Rhythms

DIRECTIONS

With hands or feet, start off with a simple rhythm, such as hopping twice on each foot. Have the player(s) do the same thing. Proceed to more complicated rhythms such as hopping twice on one foot and once on the other or three times on one foot and two times on the other. Advance to three hops on the right foot followed by one hop on the left foot and then two hops on the right. You get the idea, I hope.

Try tapping out various rhythms with your hands such as "shave and a haircut—two cents" and then break them into which hand or foot does what. For example, left hand hits thigh for the three beats of "shave and a" and then right hand does the two beats of "haircut" on the other thigh. Both hands pat head for "two cents."

If a player has a hard time, add sounds. Two hops on the right foot is accompanied by the sound "beep beep" and the one hop on the left foot goes with the sound "boop."

I've Got a Note Inside of Me

In this game, each player sings any notes and the other players imitate that pitch. Before each person's turn, the group sings, "Babsie has a note inside of her that goes like this." Then Babsie sings whatever note she feels. The group imitates it and then goes on to the next player. "Skipper has a note inside of him that goes like this." Skipper sings whatever note he has inside him and the group imitates it.

VARIATION

♦ If the kids are young, you might just want to do, "I've got a *noise* inside of me." I find that this kind of make-a-sound game is the easiest one for little kids. They may be reluctant to make movements or say their names, but have no problem making noises.

Torn Leaf

Success means everyone wins!

DIRECTIONS

This game can be played spontaneously outside. Take a leaf that is dying or damaged and tear it into as many pieces as there are people playing. Then, sit down and together try to put the leaf puzzle back in its original shape.

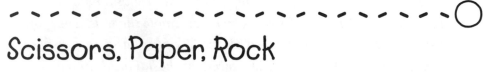

   This game can also be done with a piece of paper.

Scissors, Paper, Rock

This is how we settle little matters. Who turns off the porch light? Who goes and gets the mail? We do scissors, paper, rock. It seems as fair as flipping a coin—and a little more fun.

DIRECTIONS

Do you know the hand game called, Scissors, Paper, Rock? There are three gestures one can make. On the count of three, each partner makes one of them: scissors, using the index and third fingers; paper, using an open hand; or rock, using a fist. If both partners use the same gesture, they repeat the game. If not, one wins according to the following rules:

◇ Scissors cuts paper, so scissors wins.

◇ Paper covers rock, so paper wins.

◇ Rock smashes scissors, so rock wins.

VARIATIONS

◆ This is the *leg* version. On the count of three each player makes a gesture with their legs that is either an open wide leg stance (paper), legs straight and together (rock), or legs crossed (scissors). Same rules apply.

◆ In a group circle, the group watches as two people play. The winner skips over to the next player in the circle. Those two then play the game, and the winner skips to the next player. It might end up with one player skipping all around the circle. But probably not. The game is mostly luck.

Paper   Rock   Scissors

Turns, Turns

One of the most unpleasant realities young children have to face is the idea of taking turns. Sometimes it is much more fun to have something all to your-self for as long as you want it. Here is an activity that reinforces the idea that taking turns is all part of the game.

CHANT

Turns turns, we all take turns.

_____ (name) goes first

And _____ (name) goes next.

DIRECTIONS

Show your group an unusual object that is not too complicated. A toy that spins when you push a button, clicks when you press it, or creaks when you spin it is perfect. Hold it up; demonstrate it, and then chant together.

Example

Turns turns, we all take turns.

Bonnie goes first and Trisha goes next.

Trisha takes the toy and plays with it while the group sings:

Turns turns, we all take turns.

Trisha goes first and Monty goes next.

You might have to speed the song up or slow it down or add some words. For example, "It's hard to let go of your turn, but it's Janie's turn now. You can have another turn later."

Introductions

Social skills improve with practice. Try practicing first among family and friends.

DIRECTIONS

Family members are seated in a circle or around a table. Each gets to introduce the person sitting to the right, telling the others something about that person. For example, "This is my sister Eliza. She likes to read books and play pretend."

VARIATION

◆ Play the game with children who do not know each other very well already. You might have partners interview each other beforehand so that each has some specific information to give. For example, "This is Lorraine. She loves to wear silk clothes and hopes to be a midwife someday."

When Were You Born?

DIRECTIONS

Invite the group to form a circle. Tell the children to think about the season in which they were born: summer, spring, winter, or fall. Then demonstrate an appropriate movement for each season. For example, children born in the spring could twirl; those born in winter could stomp feet (as in getting snow off boots). Fall kids could flutter hands (as in falling leaves), and summer kids could make swimming motions.

Then go around the circle and ask each person to show what season they were born in by making one of the above movements.

VARIATIONS

♦ Go around the circle a second time and see who remembers who was born when.

♦ Have people of like birth dates get together and choreograph a dance for their season. Have them present it to the group.

Pass It on

DIRECTIONS

Pass different movements around the circle. The first child does something like shaking the hand of the child to the right and then that child shakes the hand of the next child. The handshaking continues around the circle until the second child starts a new movement such as a wink. After the wink goes around the circle, the third child starts the next movement, and so on until everyone has a turn.

Other possibilities:

◇ pinch cheeks

◇ pat back

◇ say "hello"

◇ stick out tongue

◇ throw a kiss

Sway and Bend

Getting everyone to sway in the same direction takes time, but not words. Just start the movement and eventually everyone will be in harmony.

DIRECTIONS

Hold each other's forearms while in a circle and all bend backwards, supporting each other. If that is too hard for your group, start by sitting in a circle with toes pointing straight ahead to the middle of the circle. Hold forearms and lean back.

While sitting or standing, try to all sway in the same direction so you are like blades of grass being blown back and forth by the wind.

Kangaroo

Assign each child an animal to be. Make sure that there are at least two of each type. The object is for each child to find another who is the same animal so in the end the pairs or group of animals are together. The children have to go around either making the sound of their animals, moving like their animals, or showing something about their animals. Possible animals: Kangaroo, dog, scorpion, wolf, goat, cat, elephant, deer, or cow.

VARIATION

◆ Instead of using sound, older kids can use their detective skills by asking the different players a variety of questions to tease out what kind of animals they are. Questions have to be the kind that can be answered with a Yes or No. For instance:

Do you live in the jungle?

Do you need water to survive?

Do you live alone?

Make a Sandwich

How many ingredients there are depends on the number of children. Make sure there are enough children left over to be the eaters!

DIRECTIONS

Making a sandwich is as easy as making a line. Pick a person to be the bread (or tortilla or pita bread, etc.). She stands at the line's front. The next person stands beside the bread and is the mustard. The next person is the ham, the next the cheese. Add a pickle person, some sprouts children, a little mayo person, and so on, until the sandwich is finished and the last piece of bread is at the end. Everyone else can then pretend to eat it all.

VARIATION

This same game can be played with children lying beside each other (or on top of each other!).

Hot Sand

DIRECTIONS

Ask your group to imagine themselves walking on different surfaces. As the children are walking around, ask them to imagine they are walking on the following items.

Hot sand, tacks, water, bubble gum, mud, wet grass, deep water, soft earth, peanut butter, marshmallows, pebbles, feathers, whipped cream, dry leaves, thick carpet, slick ice, sharp rocks, cement, snow, or *the moon.*

Remember to remind the children, especially the younger ones, to "walk into the empty spaces" to keep them from bumping into each other.

Walk Like

DIRECTIONS

Ask your players to walk as if they were different characters or creatures. Here are a few to try:

Giant, tennis player, fairy, thief, baby, old man, soldier, swimmer, bullfighter, king, queen, robot, ballerina, clown, dragon, eagle, shark, butterfly, frog, amoeba, centipede, lion, mouse, hippo, camel, kangaroo, tick, dog, sand crab, witch, rock star, moth.

Act Like

DIRECTIONS

Ask your players to move as if they were these different things:

Waterfall, ocean, mountain, television, toaster, explosion, sailboat, book, accordion, refrigerator, fireplace, gate, popcorn popper, windshield wiper, telephone, washing machine, dishwasher, satellite dish, blimp, sand dune, river, yo-yo, hurricane.

Move Like

DIRECTIONS

Ask your players how these sounds would look in movement:

◇ Moo

◇ Meow

◇ Screech

◇ Choo choo

◇ Ha! ha! ha! (laughing)

◇ Boo hoo (crying)

◇ Bong bong

◇ Tongue click

◇ Raspberry

Run Like

DIRECTIONS

Ask your players to run as if they were in these different situations:

◇ A monster is chasing you.

◇ You are a baby.

◇ You are very old.

◇ You are an ocean wave.

◇ You are a teenage boy.

◇ You are an old lady in a hurry.

◇ You are carrying a bucket of milk.

Riding

DIRECTIONS

Ask your children to act as if they were taking a ride on one of the following: *Canoe, kayak, white water raft, space ship, monorail, witches broom, wagon, sports car, horse, motorcycle, subway, camel, rainbow, magic carpet,* or *Conestoga wagon.*

Pretty Butterfly

SONG

I am a pretty butterfly, butterfly, butterfly.

I am a pretty butterfly—fly, fly, fly.

I am a green grasshopper, grasshopper, grasshopper.

I am a green grasshopper—hop, hop, hop.

I am a red fire engine, fire engine.

I am a red fire engine—steer, steer, steer.

I am a little baby, baby, baby.

I am a little baby, crawl, crawl, crawl.

DIRECTIONS

For little ones, sing this song, to the tune of your choice, and let them move however they are moved to move!

Partner Play

DIRECTIONS

Help the children form pairs. Write each of the following scenarios on a slip of paper so the partners can pick one to act out.

◇ Movie star being made up by make-up artist

◇ Ballet student being taught by teacher

◇ Saleslady helping person buying a hat

◇ Rock star being approached by a fan

◇ Barber giving a customer a shave and a haircut

◇ Kids cleaning a window, one on each side

Duck Walk

DIRECTIONS

If your children would like specific directions on ways to "move like an animal," here are some suggestions that are fun to try:

◇ Duck walk: Squat down, lace hands behind back to form a tail.

◇ Crab walk: Sitting on the floor with knees bent and feet flat on floor, lean back on arms and lift bottom off ground. Walk sideways, keeping body and head in straight line.

◇ Frog jump: Squat down with hands placed well in front of body between legs. Move forward to hands. Move hands forward again.

◇ Kangaroo hop: In a standing position, place feet together and hands at chest level for paws. Jump around, keeping feet together.

◇ Elephant walk: Bend forward at hips, put hands together with arms extended for trunk. Walk forward with knees stiff, swaying arms (the trunk) side to side.

◇ Lobster walk: Sitting on the floor with knees bent, feet flat on floor, lean back on arms and lift bottom off ground. Walk backwards toward hands. Then move hands backwards.

◇ Inchworm glide: Bend forward to touch both hands to the ground, keeping knees and elbows stiff, walk hands forward, then walk feet to hands with knees inside elbows.

◇ Chicken walk: In a squat position with feet together and knees apart, grasp ankles (left hand to left ankle) with arms inside knees. Walk forward in this position clucking like a chicken.

◇ Bunny hop: In a squat position with hands placed outside knees, move hands forward, then hop forward to them.

◇ Seal walk: Body prone. Hands on floor, fingers turned outward and back so heels of hands forward. Arms straight so head and chest is lifted off the ground. Pull body forward just using hands.

Rocking Chair

DIRECTIONS

Ask your group to be different things! Here are a few ways to try:

◇ Rocking chair: While sitting, grasp ankles and rock body forward and backward, or side to side, or around in a circle.

◇ Flower: Start in a bent-over squat position and slowly unbend, straightening head, body, arms, and legs to a standing position with arms stretched overhead. Reverse movement to make drooping flower that, after you give it water, stands up straight again.

◇ Snowball: Child curls up as if a ball, with arms wrapped around legs, then rolls around (or you roll the child in various directions).

◇ Windshield wipers: With arms in front of body, elbows bent at 90 degrees and fingers pointing up, rotate upper arms so lower arms and hands move from side to side.

◇ Elevator: Stand with trunk erect. Then squat down, keeping trunk erect, then stand up again. Adding words such as "going down," "third floor," "basement," stop partway up or down.

◇ Pepper mill: Place one hand on floor with arm straight; place the other hand on hip. Walk around using the extended arm as a pivot point.

Animals, Plants, Insects, and Cars

DIRECTIONS

Set up different scenarios for the children to demonstrate:

◇ A dog chasing a ball

◇ A cat stretching

◇ A plant growing

◇ A flower opening up

◇ A tree blowing in the wind

◇ A weeping willow tree

◇ A fly buzzing about

◇ A butterfly going from flower to flower

◇ A grasshopper jumping

◇ A tow truck towing

◇ A bulldozer digging

◇ A public bus picking up passengers

Plain Pretend

For little ones, too many choices can be confusing. Keep it simple!

DIRECTIONS

Even very young children understand these simple scenarios. Help your group act out the following:

◇ I am a bird, I can fly.

◇ I'm an airplane, I can soar.

◇ I am a dog, I can bark.

◇ I am a kangaroo, I can jump!

Be a Tree

DIRECTIONS

Help your group imagine and act out the growth of a tree as you narrate its story from an acorn to a mighty oak. Describe the oak as it goes through various days such as a breezy day, a stormy day, a hot day. Sadly, let the tree be chopped down or grow old and fall over in a storm. Then imagine it rotted away, making a lovely home for termites.

Make a Machine

DIRECTIONS

One child starts this game by standing in front of the group, making a movement with her body but keeping her feet stationary; any movement will do. The next person goes and stands near the first and makes a movement that relates to the first person's. There are no rules. Anything that seems to make sense to the child is good enough. Then each child who wants to play joins the group, one by one, adding their input. The children who are left and watching then name the machine or imagine how to use it.

VARIATION

♦ Tell the children ahead of time what kind of machine they are making, such as a washing machine or a printing press.

Occupations

Imagine what people do who have different occupations. Sometimes kids need a little help to do this. So, if they ask, I take them aside and whisper an idea or two in their ears. For example, a carpenter would pick up a piece of board, measure it, saw it, hammer it.

DIRECTIONS

Each child who wants to can take a turn standing in front of the group to act out the duties of any occupation. The others get to call out what occupations they think it is.

Possible occupations:

Ballerina, reggae musician, astronaut, king, queen, tennis player, bull-fighter, president, thief, football player, carnival person, swimmer, teacher, politician, clown, surfer, farmer, or baseball player.

VARIATION

♦ Rather than guessing out loud, group members, one by one, join the actor and do their version of that occupation. For example, if one child got up and started "nailing boards," another might join in miming sawing a board or measuring.

Act Out a Situation

DIRECTIONS

Ask the children to act as if they were having these different experiences by showing the emotions they would feel. You can write each experience down on a slip of paper and let the players choose:

◇ Need to pee, badly, in the middle of downtown, and nobody will let you use their bathroom

◇ Lost and hungry in the woods at night

◇ Starring in a Shakespeare performance—it's opening night and you can't remember your lines

◇ Feeling fat and have to lead aerobics class

◇ Sailing a ship during a storm and the rudder breaks

◇ Being burned at the stake as a malevolent witch and you know you're kind and innocent

◇ Waking up to find you are in a s-l-o-w motion movie

◇ Trying to catch a toad who keeps hopping away

◇ Holding a crying baby for the first time in your life

◇ With a sprained ankle, trying to run from a mugger

◇ Carrying a bowl of hot soup when a rat runs across your path

◇ Trying to sneak up some creaky stairs and not wake your parents

◇ Walking on what starts off as a windy day, then turns into a hot scorching day, and ends up to be a rainy, stormy day

Story Time

Write this "story" down as it's being told and then read it back to the group.

DIRECTIONS

The children sit in a circle. One starts a story, for example, "Once there was a wicked witch who liked to eat . . ." The next person adds a sentence or two that furthers the story, for example ". . . pink fuzzy geraniums, but one day when she went to pick the pink fuzzy geraniums, she found . . ." Then it's the next person's turn.

VARIATIONS

♦ If the children are older and the group is small, encourage everyone to go on longer than just a sentence or two. Challenge each person to create a mini-adventure to leave hanging for the next person.

♦ Each player adds just one word.

Act Out Nursery Rhymes

DIRECTIONS

For a group of younger children, tell a simple nursery rhyme, then invite the children to act it. Ask one or two questions that will help the children imagine what to do.

Examples

◇ How did Jack and Jill look climbing the hill? Show me how they tumbled down it.

◇ How does Little Miss Muffet look when she sits on her tuffet? How does the spider walk up beside her?

VARIATION

♦ Encourage children to make up and act out longer endings to familiar nursery rhymes. Here are some questions to stimulate the children's imaginations:

What happened after Jack and Jill got up? How did they look walking home?

What happened to Humpty Dumpty? What did all the King's men do later?

What did the spider do with Miss Muffet's curds and whey?

Act Out a Story

DIRECTIONS

Invite older children to act out simple tales such as "The Three Pigs" or "Little Red Riding Hood." Divide the group in two. Have the first group act out a familiar story, with the second group playing the audience. Part way through, have the first group be the audience while the second group takes over the acting. Switch back and forth as often as the group can handle the change. Let players take different parts each time.

Act Out Action

DIRECTIONS

Have the children write down ideas for all kinds of actions. Put each idea on a strip of paper. Each player picks one and acts out the action described. Some possibilities:

Materials
Pencils and paper

◇ Washing dishes

◇ Sweeping a floor

◇ Nursing a baby

◇ Walking a tightrope

◇ Taking care of new puppy

Others have to guess the action being performed.

Play Pretend

DIRECTIONS

Give your group a series of scenarios to act out quickly. Clap your hands whenever you want one scenario to end, and call out another to start.

- ◇ Drinking tea at a tea party
- ◇ Making and eating toasted marshmallows around a campfire
- ◇ Being a lion tamer
- ◇ Doing an underwater ballet
- ◇ Playing in a rock band
- ◇ Playing in an orchestra
- ◇ Chopping wood
- ◇ Exploring a jungle
- ◇ Eating corn on the cob
- ◇ Driving a tractor

Changing Ball

DIRECTIONS

Stand in a circle and pretend to throw a ball around the circle, continually changing the kind of ball it is. Pretend it's a balloon, then a beach ball, then a basketball, then a bowling ball, then a tennis ball, then a baseball, then a golf ball, then a Ping-Pong ball.

VARIATIONS

- ◆ What about changing the temperature of the ball? Sometimes it's hot, sometimes ice cold.

♦ Players each change the nature of the ball. One says it's a sticky slimy ball. The person who catches the slime ball says she changed it into a marble and flicks it to the next person. He changes it into a fluff ball and blows it to the next person, and so on.

♦ Players each make a sound when they catch the "ball." Remind them not to plan their sound, but to release whatever sound comes out when the ball comes toward them.

♦ Imagine the ball keeps changing except there is no limitation on what it can be. It does not always need to be a ball. As it passes from child to child, each can change it from ball to a flower to a tube of lipstick to a telephone to a handkerchief, and so on.

Opening Lines

DIRECTIONS

Invite the children to do improvisations based on the opening lines you give them. Possible opening lines are:

◇ I smell smoke.

◇ Surprise!

◇ Call an ambulance.

◇ The car won't start.

◇ I am afraid of height.

◇ I'm never coming here again.

◇ How could you!

◇ Stop!!!

Opening Idea

Given enough time, older children can make whole plays.

DIRECTIONS

Let kids form groups to make plays. Each groups gets to choose from these opening ideas:

◇ Rip Van Winkle awakes after 100 years.

◇ It's 4 A.M. on a dark and stormy night, and someone is knocking at the door.

◇ You hear a baby crying for a long time in the apartment next door. You go to check, but the door is locked.

◇ Radio announcer says, "Aliens have landed."

◇ Gravity has suddenly stopped working.

Going to Mexico

This is a memory game. When I played it in a Spanish class, I had to say the items in Spanish.

DIRECTIONS

Children sit in a circle. The first person says, "I am going to Mexico, and I am taking a . . . ," naming or acting out something that would be good to take. The next person says the same line, says or acts out what the first person said, and adds an item to the list. The third person then repeats what the first two are taking and adds a third, and the game continues for as many rounds as the group can handle.

Tug of War

Remember to keep that rope taut!

DIRECTIONS

Form two teams. Using a "space rope," that is, an imaginary rope, the teams take sides and try to pull each other over the imaginary line. Or start with two players and keep adding more.

Fortunately, Unfortunately

DIRECTIONS

The group makes up a story one sentence at a time, in which the first word of the first sentence is "unfortunately." The next player adds the second sentence, beginning with the word "fortunately." Then the next person takes over, starting with the word "unfortunately."

Continue the story with each person adding on and alternating the first word from "fortunately" to "unfortunately."

Example

"Unfortunately, when I walked down the street, I fell in a manhole."

"Fortunately, the manhole had water inside so I didn't hurt myself when I fell."

"Unfortunately, the water had rats swimming it."

"Fortunately, the water ran swiftly and soon I was swept out to the ocean."

"Unfortunately, the ocean was full of sharks."

"Fortunately, a boat came by and picked me up."

"Unfortunately, there were pirates on the ship."

What's Happening Now?

Children grow from the experience of sharing the little things, good and bad, that happen any day.

DIRECTIONS

Enjoy taking turns acting out everyday events. Others have to guess what's happening. For example:

◇ Washing dishes

◇ Breaking a glass and cleaning it up

◇ Getting new skates, putting them on, falling down a lot, and then getting better and skating

Foreign Greetings

My family once lived on an island where raising one's eyebrows was a form of recognition, a greeting to strangers and friends alike. When we returned to America over a year later and went to a grocery store, my then ten-year-old daughter said, "People are so rude here—nobody even once raised their eyebrows at me!"

In this game, players act out different cultures' ways of greeting each other.

DIRECTIONS

Players walk toward each other, do one of the following, and then walk on:

- ◇ Nod head (America)
- ◇ Bow head with hands in prayer gesture (India)
- ◇ Bow from waist (Japan)
- ◇ Kowtow on knees (ancient China)
- ◇ Curtsy (England)
- ◇ Kiss both cheeks (France)
- ◇ Raise eyebrows (Micronesia)

VARIATION

- ◆ Make up gestures or types of handshakes as if your group were forming a new country and had to make up new forms of greeting.

Ishkibibble Talk

DIRECTIONS

Children pretend they are from the planet of Ishkibibble (or planet of your choice) and they have come to Earth to buy something specific. Through the use of gibberish and gestures, they must explain what they want to a store clerk who does not speak their language. Possible items to buy:

Ballet shoes, car jack, motor oil, chain saw, bird cage, stapler, curtain, antennae, spaghetti, lipstick, candy bar, bug spray, sunglasses.

Children take turns playing the alien and the store clerk while the others watch.

Soda Pop

How does food move? Stretch your players' imaginations. It's fun to see what kids come up with for this game!

DIRECTIONS

Have children move like the following foods or make up others:

◇ Soda pop
◇ Molasses or honey
◇ Gelatin
◇ Bread rising
◇ Peas

◇ Bubble gum
◇ Noodles, stiff and then cooked
◇ Peanut butter
◇ Popcorn
◇ Ice cream melting

What Else Can It Be?

CHANT

A stick, a stick, what else can it be?

DIRECTIONS

Sit in a circle and pass around any common object—a stick, for example—and chant before each person's turn.

Maybe, through words and movements, the first kid will turn it into a toothbrush, another into an ear of corn. One might show the stick being a baton, another a stick of dynamite.

When no one can think of anything new, introduce a new object such as a piece of paper. Saying the chant in between turns, watch a paper napkin, for instance, turn into a face cloth, a hat, a shield, a piece of bread, and so on.

Materials

Common household items

Chapter 9

LEARNING TO TRUST

How much we trust others depends a lot on our experiences in life, especially how we were treated as children. In some cases, a healthy distrust is appropriate. These games encourage the opposite.

Willow in Wind

DIRECTIONS

Have the group form a tight circle with one child in the center. Direct her to keep her back straight and fall to the side, back, or front while the others catch her with their hands and push her back to center. Each person gets a turn in the center, falling two to three times. This game is a little scary at first but is always surprisingly fun. Keep the circle tight and close in for the beginning tries and then as the players get braver and more trusting, tell everyone to take one or two steps back!

Spread-Eagle Carry

DIRECTIONS

While lying on his back, one child allows himself to be picked up by a group of kids, each of whom is responsible for supporting him in a special way. Someone supports his head, another his shoulders, another his body, another his legs, and so on.

VARIATION

♦ The child is lying face down when picked up.

The Synchronized Walk

This game encourages children to be very aware of each other. My daughter and her friends—two girls and a boy with different size strides—played it one day by taking turns matching each other's stride. They remarked to me later that it felt really nice to be walking in sync with each other and to feel how the others moved.

DIRECTIONS

Divide the children into groups of two or four. Tell each group to walk together with arms at sides and arms and hips touching, so that they move as a unit. The challenge is to walk at the exact same speed, taking the same size steps.

Dominoes

This is a game that any sane adult would avoid, but children seem to think it's great silly fun. Surprisingly, I've never seen anyone get hurt. I think children like the opportunity to be physically close to each other, and this provides an opportunity that is not as intimate and vulnerable as hugging. Explain the game ahead of time and give children the chance to opt out if they want to.

DIRECTIONS

Line the kids up, each one standing very closely behind the next on a thick mat. Then, push the first one down. That will make the next one fall, which will make the next one fall, and so on.

Scramble

If you have a small group and a large room containing heavy furniture, such as tables, a desk, a sofa, or game equipment, you can plan this very friendly "touchy" game.

DIRECTIONS

Call out the name of a piece of furniture. Everyone has to scramble onto it, clutching each other until everyone fits. If everyone can stay on at the same time, they are winners!

Color Touching

DIRECTIONS

Ask the group to form a close circle, then ask them to reach out with their right hands and touch something blue on someone's clothes. With their left hands, have them touch something red. Then, if the mood is right or you want to lighten things up, ask them to reach out with their right or left feet while their hands are still touching the appropriate spots. At this point, ask them to touch something green. They should be in a hopeless tangle by now, so what's the difference if you also add, "and with your head . . ."

Reflections

Trust between people who are working together grows whenever one imitates the other. There is something about moving in sync that makes a person feel understood.

DIRECTIONS

Two people stand facing each other. One is to be a reflection of the other. The first person starts moving very slowly, as if standing in front of a mirror practicing different arms, body, and leg movements. The reflection person tries to imitate those movements. Encourage the children to keep eye contact while using their peripheral vision to see the movements.

When you say "Reverse," or when they feel ready, they should switch— the one who was leader takes a turn being the reflection.

As children get better and better at this activity, they learn to move slowly and watch each other closely.

Walk and Look

Keep moving as you chant, and the children will follow.

CHANT

I look and I look
And I see _____.

DIRECTIONS

At first, have the group walk around the room looking at nothing in particular while you chant repetitively: "I look and I look and I see very little."

Then change the chant to "I look and I look and I see *things*." The players call out things they see, such as a red scarf, a turquoise necklace, brown shoes, a green rug.

Then change the chant to "I look and I look and I see you." On the word "you," the players make eye contact with whoever they are nearest for a brief moment until you start the chant again, after which they look at another person.

After a while, change the chant to "I look and I look and I touch you." The players touch the person they are nearest on the word "you."

End the session with "I look and I look and I hug you." How long you pause between repetitions depends upon how comfortable your group is with looking at, touching, and hugging each other.

VARIATION

♦ If your group is ready for feedback, have them stop after the chant "I see you," and tell the person that they see what they notice. Maybe it's something the person has on, a look in her eyes, the style of her hair, or her posture.

Trust Fall

DIRECTIONS

Form pairs and stand facing each other, arms slightly bent and palms touching. Experiment with leaning away from each other then coming toward each other, touching palms.

Then take a step or two backward with arms still flexed and palms outward, and lean toward each other, catching each other with palms. Do that a few times until comfortable and then try it with eyes closed. Then try it with turning in a circle and falling forward, catching each other, safely, with your palms!

The Arm Carry

Being carried does more than evoke a sense of trust; it also brings back pleasant childhood memories. As we get older, we have to foster our independence. So it's nice, for brief periods, to allow ourselves to be "babied" again.

DIRECTIONS

Form a team of three children, two to be carriers and one to be carried.

Start with the two carriers putting their arms out straight toward each other. Then each puts his right hand on top of his left elbow joint. Then, with left hands, each grabs the other's arm just above the bent elbow, forming a square.

The third child gets to sit inside the square and put an arm around the neck of each carrier.

The Sideways Carry

This is an amazingly secure carry and one that little people can do with bigger, heavier people. My 5'4" daughter picks up all 5'6" of me and is happy to walk me around. She would even twirl me if I weren't squealing to be let down.

DIRECTIONS

The carrier stands besides the person she is going to carry and puts her arm around his waist so they are both facing the same direction. Then she puts her leg in front of and to the side of both his legs so that his body is now perpendicular to her back. She then bends over and picks him up, holding his legs to get a more secure hold.

Back to Back Carry

This is a good way to have your back nicely stretched. It's used in some dance classes during warm-ups, so remind the person being carried to relax and allow the stretch.

DIRECTIONS

Match up pairs in which at least one partner, the carrier, can support the other's weight. Each couple stands back to back with their arms straight up above their heads. The carrier grabs the other person's wrists and then leans over until the feet of the person being carried cannot touch the ground.

Piggy Back

If you want to see smiles, this activity is sure to produce them.

DIRECTIONS

Match pairs so one person can ride on the back of another like a rider on a horse, legs wrapped around the waist of the "horsey" and arms around the neck.

Group Walk

DIRECTIONS

Players line up and wrap their arms around the person or persons in front of them and walk forward, backward, and sideways as you direct or as they decide.

VARIATION

♦ While joined together, the players act out the following scenario:

Looking for a home (walking forward), jumping a creek (jump on count of three), climbing a mountain (taking high steps as in marching), getting tired (partly squatting), and going to sleep (lying on side "spooning" each other and snoring).

Chapter 10

EXPRESSING AFFECTION

What we want for our children is the same as what we want for ourselves. For most of us, that means a satisfying and fulfilling life with people we love and who love us, and a sense that our lives were worthwhile. These games will give you lots of easy ways to show affection and regard.

Just-Because Hug

People never outgrow their need to be touched affectionately. When I was a young adult, I was standing with my aunt in the kitchen talking and suddenly, for no apparent reason, she reached over and gave me a good hug. A feeling of love came over her and she acted upon it. How wonderful that made me feel—to be hugged for no reason other than for being myself!

DIRECTIONS

Give your child a friendly, loving, just-because-you-are-you hug.

Just-Because Compliment

There are other ways we can show our affection besides hugging and kissing. We can do it by appreciating our children's essence and not just their accomplishments. Often, children get the feeling that we praise them only when they produce—get a good grade in school, draw a lovely picture, make a touchdown. Without praise for just being themselves, they can grow up feeling compelled to accomplish and yet never feel satisfied by their accomplishments. Strangers can compliment a child for their products, but parents must also show that they love their child just "for being you."

DIRECTIONS

Listen to your child. Over time, try to discover what personal qualities he or she is proud of having. Find ways to recognize and compliment those qualities.

Mess Around

Spending time doing things together is another way of expressing affection. We are the people our children love the most; if they see that we like to do things with them, they will grow up knowing they are valued companions.

DIRECTIONS

For a few minutes each day, take time to go for a walk, play a game, mess around on the piano, or look at clouds. Do any friendly activity that you and your child enjoy together but tend to forget about in the mass of everyday things that need doing.

How Do You Dos

One day I was hauling my four-year-old daughter around as I did errands in town. She followed quietly beside me as I spoke to various people along the way. Later, I realized that I hadn't introduced her to them. I had acted as if I were alone and she a nonentity. I remembered times when new company had come over to the house. I treated my kids like background noise, never acknowledging that their increased noise was their way of trying to be noticed. (I have noticed, by the way, that the way to get kids to be quiet is to introduce them. Suddenly they become tongue-tied the way many adults do when they meet celebrities!) Introducing children is a way of showing them that they are important enough to be recognized.

DIRECTIONS

Practice introductions with your child, as if you were playing a game, so he knows how you would want him to respond to a real introduction. Take turns being the introducer and the person being introduced. Then, whenever you have an opportunity, introduce your child to someone who you know will enjoy the occasion.

I Like You

As you are snuggling your children to sleep or checking on them in the night, you can whisper to them how wonderful, beautiful, brave, smart, and lovely they are. You can say whatever is in your heart. When you look upon those sweet dear faces in repose, it is not hard to find the words.

Sometimes, it's hard to be as open about your feelings when your children are wide awake! At those times, it can be easier to express what's in your heart in song.

SONG

I like you.

There's no doubt about it—

I like you.

There's no doubt about it—

I like you.

There's no doubt about it.

We are such good friends.

DIRECTIONS

This song is one of my favorites for expressing affection. I don't remember how I learned it—I might have even made it up. Feel free to make up your own tune. The words are easy in any language.

VARIATION

◆ Try signing the words. I really like the sign for "friends." It's two interlocking index fingers.

Go on to the second and third verses. Often, children want to hear more. The rest goes like this:

You like me.

There's no doubt about it—

You like me.

There's no doubt about it.

We are such good friends.

We both like each other.

There's no doubt about it—

We both like each other.

There's no doubt about it.

WE ARE SUCH GOOD FRIENDS!

If You're Happy and You Know It

This is not an affection song, but it is filled with such joy that anyone who sings it feels affection for the world.

SONG

If you're happy and you know it,

(blink your eyes).

If you're happy and you know it,

(snort your nose).

If you're happy and you know it,

And you really want to show it,

If you're happy and you know it,

(Shout boobadeboop).

DIRECTIONS

If you've sung the original song, then you know the standard variations of showing happiness—shouting "hurrah" and stamping your feet and clapping your hands. I find it more enlivening to have children make up other ways, such as blinking, snorting, shouting "boobadeba," to express joy their way.

For a large group of children, divide them into small groups of three and let each group make up a sound—any sound. Try to encourage, by example, original or silly sounds rather than, say, a dog bark or cat meow, because the unexpected makes everyone laugh. When the song goes "If you're happy and you know it, say _____," point to one of the groups to make their sound. Point to a different group for each verse, sometimes pointing to more than one group at a time. At the end, have everyone make all the sounds at the same time.

VARIATION

♦ You don't really need a lot of people for this game. A "group" can also be just you and your child.

Love

I've been told that this is how Isadora Duncan, the famous modern dancer, ended her classes. Don't underestimate the effect on your children of small traditions.

CHANT

From my heart to the sky,

From my heart to the earth,

From my heart to everyone.

DIRECTIONS

Put your hands over your hearts and say together "From my heart to the sky." As you speak, reach from heart to sky; then back to heart.

Then say, "From my heart to the earth," reaching from heart toward earth, then back to heart.

Finish by saying, "From my heart to everyone," with your arms going out to the side. If this is done in a circle, it's nice to encircle the waists of the people on either side.

VARIATION

◆ Make one of the gestures a secret message between you and your child. When you leave him at his friend's house or you see each other across the room at a group gathering, you can touch your heart and then open your hand to him. He can respond in kind. It's like blowing a kiss but much more private.

Good-bye

If you have been playing with a group of children and want to bring closure to the day, or if you just want to have your own family's way of saying good-bye, try a song.

SONG

(To the tune of "Good Night, Ladies")

Good-bye _____ (child's name),

Good-bye _____ (another child's name),

Good bye _____ (a parent's name),

We hate to see you go.

Boom boom boom!

Good-bye _____ (the dog's name),

Good-bye _____ (the cat's name),

Good-bye everyone,

Now it's time to go.

Boom Boom!

DIRECTIONS

Repeat the first verse until you mention everyone or everything you need to include. They may be favorite stuffed animals and dolls, friends, neighbors, and even the house itself.

VARIATION

♦ If you are saying good-bye to your child or children, exchange the words "Now it's time to go" for the exact time you'll see each other. For example, "I'll see you in twenty minutes," or "I'll see you after lunch."

Group Hug

There is nothing quite like being part of a group and feeling very included. Group hugs can give children that feeling anywhere, at any time, for any reason.

DIRECTIONS

Just start to hug each other and welcome others to join in the embrace, arms around waists or shoulders.

CLOSING THOUGHTS

We try to be good parents and do what's best for our children. Sometimes we succeed, and sometimes we only succeed some.

I am reminded of a little skit one of my daughters did when she was ten, near the end of that time when your kids still think you're great. She called it "The Perfect Mom," and it was all about how hard it was to have a perfect mom. For instance, she missed out on complaining with her friends about what a drag her mom was. She missed out on a good rebellion because her mom was too accommodating, and so on.

However, she went on to say that maybe the perfect mom actually wasn't all that perfect. She didn't really enjoy cooking that much, and she wasn't all that good at it. She was a little lazy. She ironed her clothes by just wetting them and hanging them up, letting gravity do the work. There were other little complaints.

Hmmm, she thought at the end. Maybe her mom wasn't perfect. Perhaps someday she would find the perfect mom, she concluded, "and maybe—just maybe—it will be me!"

We don't need to be perfect parents. We just need to enjoy, appreciate, and love our children and pass some of our own good traits down the line.

Index

⋏ highlights activities that are tailored for children who are five and under. ◯ signals activities that are good for groups.